THE MIDDLE AGES

Like the knights of Europe, who knew nothing of their distant
land, the *samurai* warriors of Japan wore splendid armor (above).

HISTORICAL FACTS
THE MIDDLE AGES

RICHARD O'NEILL

Peasants gather grapes in September: from the *Très Riches Heures* of the Duke of Berry, famous illustrated manuscript of the 15th century.

Art and engineering skill are united in a Renaissance master work: Brunelleschi's octagonal dome (completed 1436) for Florence Cathedral.

CRESCENT BOOKS
NEW YORK • AVENEL, NEW JERSEY

CLB 2838

© 1992 Colour Library Books Ltd., Godalming, Surrey, England.

This 1992 edition published by Crescent Books,
distributed by Outlet Book Company, Inc.,
a Random House Company
40 Engelhard Avenue, Avenel, New Jersey 07001

Printed and bound in Italy

ISBN 0 517 06565 7

8 7 6 5 4 3 2 1

The Author
Richard O'Neill was born in Northampton, England. He has been a soldier,
professional boxer, laborer, actor, and writer of fiction, comic strips, and
stage and television plays. In recent years he has specialized in historical
non-fiction. His book *Suicide Squads: Special Attack Weapons of World War II*
was published in Britain and the U.S.A. in 1981, and in Japan in 1988. He is
co-author of two books on toy collecting, and has edited and contributed to
many books on military history and weaponry. He was a major contributor to
Lands and Peoples, a multi-volume work published in the U.S.A. and other
countries in 1990-92. He is currently writing a book on the Middle Ages,
two books on ghosts, monsters, and similar phenomena, and working on a
movie project with his son Danny, an actor and director.

Credits
Editor: Richard O'Neill
Designer: Jill Coote
Map artwork: Peter Bull
Picture Editor: Miriam Sharland
Production: Ruth Arthur, Sally Connolly, Andrew Whitelaw
Director of Production: Gerald Hughes
Typesetting: SX Composing Ltd.
Color separations: Scantrans Pte Ltd., Singapore
Printed and bound by New Interlitho SpA, Italy

A potent symbol of the power of feudal rulers, Caerphilly
Castle, Wales, was built by Gilbert de Clare, Norman overlord
of Glamorgan, in c.1270-1300.

CONTENTS

Introduction

History's Middle Ages are generally agreed to begin with the collapse of the Roman Empire in the West after A.D. 400. This marked the end of the ancient, or classical, world. The end of the Middle Ages is sometimes dated to the capture of Constantinople (modern Istanbul), capital of the Byzantine (Eastern Roman) Empire, by the Ottoman Turks. The city that had been Christianity's eastern bulwark for one thousand years fell to the Muslims on May 29, 1453, which has been memorably called 'the last day of the old world.' But most people choose, as I have done, to date the end of the old world to the 'discovery' of the New World, the Americas, in 1492.

Historians often used to call the earlier Middle Ages (roughly from c.400 through 1100) the 'Dark Ages;' not because they were any more barbarous and violent than the centuries before (or after), but because knowledge of them was obscured by lack of reliable sources. Modern research has shed more light on the period, and the negative sounding term is no longer common.

However, much of our knowledge of the Middle Ages – particularly of the personal characters and behavior of the 'great' men and women who shaped them – relies on the chroniclers (historians) of the time. Like modern journalists, they often preferred a good story to the literal truth, and were keen to make propaganda for their patrons. Thus the period is rich in legends. I have included some of the best known or most interesting and amusing – usually introducing them with the words 'it is said,' or some similar indication. It is worth remembering that most legends contain at least a grain of truth.

It is common today to hear the word 'medieval' ('of the Middle Ages') used to mean uncivilized or backward – usually by politicians or social theorists. I hope this book shows that the Middle Ages had

The ruler of the Ottoman Turks directs his army in the siege of a European city. Cannon stand ready to batter down the defensive walls, as they did at Constantinople in 1453.

no greater share of these faults than the modern world. If civilization means law and order, no modern society matches up to Genghis Khan's China in the 13th century, when it was said that if a virgin with a bag of gold walked alone across the Mongol Empire, both would end the journey intact. If it means culture, Florence under the Medici family in the 15th century beats any modern city. If it means scientific and technological progress, no modern discovery (even in the field of medicine) has benefited humanity more than the medieval invention of the printing press.

It is true that Genghis murdered millions in his conquests; that the Medici were despots kept in power by their wealth; that most ordinary people, even if able to read, could not afford the books produced by medieval printers. But the age of Hitler, Stalin, and Pol Pot; of a market economy that sees millions homeless and starving (not all in the Third World); and of increasingly unstable nations, authoritarian and democratic alike, has little cause to condemn the 'backwardness' of the Middle Ages.

'The past is another country; they do things differently there.' The popular view of the Middle Ages is of a time when kings, nobles, and the Church had all the power; when knights in armor clanked around on horseback, fighting incessant wars; when outlaws made merry in the greenwood;

LA SAVLT. DE. BEAVVAIS.

Old and new methods of warfare are united as a Burgundian army assaults Beauvais in 1472: a knight in armor directs an army of spearmen – but they are supported by light cannon.

The development of book printing, seen here in a 16th century woodcut, would spread learning to all classes.

The banker Cosimo de'Medici (1389-1464) used his wealth to make his family rulers of the city-state of Florence – and to encourage the arts on a scale seldom since excelled.

when peasants sweated, starved, and died of plague; and when women were downtrodden. And these things are true; but not the whole truth.

As this book shows, kings who abused their power were often swiftly dethroned. Powerful nobles tended to keep each other in check. Wars, although long, often involved very little combat (the English Wars of the Roses lasted 30 years, but included only about 13 weeks' fighting) between quite small armies and left most non-combatants, and the environment, undamaged. As many battles were won by ordinary soldiers with bows or pole weapons as by colorful cavalrymen. Peasants sometimes rose against their masters (rarely with much success), but except in times of famine or plague (which hit rich and poor alike) their lot in many parts of Western Europe was no worse than that of laboring folk in the 19th century. Women did suffer sexual discrimination – but strongminded women of all classes achieved great power: from queens like Theodora (*pages 16-17*) and Margaret of Anjou (*pages 92-93*) to peasants like Joan of Arc (*pages 72-73*).

A company that has ridden into immortality: some of the pilgrims of Chaucer's *Canterbury Tales*, printed by Caxton in the late 15th century, set out on their journey from London.

To read such works as *Piers the Plowman* by William Langland (c.1332-1400) or the *Canterbury Tales* of Geoffrey Chaucer (c.1340-1400) is to realize that ordinary medieval people were very much like their modern equivalents. Chaucer's Pardoner, a drummer pushing fake relics; his raunchy Wife of Bath, six times married ('not counting other company when young'); his snobbish Prioress (head woman of a nunnery), macho Miller, and gentle, intellectual Knight, are all recognizable modern types.

Piers the Plowman is a complex religious allegory, but contains magnificent and hilarious pictures of peasant life (Langland was a poor man, a minor clergyman) – as when Gluttony, on his way to church, is led astray by Betty the alewife. In the tavern he finds Cissie the shoemaker, Wat the gamekeeper and his wife, Clarice the whore (with the parish clerk), Father Peter from the abbey, a fiddler, a ratcatcher, and a host of others. He quarrels over a gambling game, drinks a huge amount of ale, staggers home 'like a blind minstrel's bitch,' sleeps for two days, and wakes with the words: 'Who's got the tankard?'

The world these folk lived in was, however, very unlike our own. The most obvious difference is that there were far fewer people in it. (The following figures are approximate, derived from reliable sources.) The world's population in A.D. 1 was around 255,000,000, of which Europe had 40,000,000. World population was only a little higher in A.D. 1000, but Europe then had 60,000,000. By 1300 the world had 430,000,000 people; Europe 73,000,000 – which was to plunge to c.50,000,000 by 1360 as a result of the 'Black Death' (*pages 74-75*). Europe's population returned to something like the 1300 figure by 1500, when the world's population was some 460,000,000 (today, it is estimated above 5,300,000,000).

Today, in the more advantaged countries, a man or woman may confidently expect a life span of

Doctors attend a sick nobleman; an illustration from a 15th century French manuscript. Medieval physicians were better skilled in the treatment of wounds than that of disease.

more than 70 years. It is difficult to compute an average life expectancy for medieval people. Life expectancy in Britain in A.D. 500 has been estimated at 33 years for a man; 27 years for a woman. Reliable figures show that as late as the 16th century only about one in ten persons in the prosperous British city of York lived beyond the age of 40. Throughout the period, men tended to have a greater life expectancy than women (today the reverse is true). It was the general custom to marry young and to have large families, and women often died in childbirth.

Outcasts of society: a leper (with red smock, warning bell, and alms bowl) and cripple are denied entrance to a town.

A study of the female anatomy by Leonardo da Vinci, who may have risked death in his quest to extend humanity's knowledge.

Medieval public and personal hygiene was generally poor. Emperor Frederick II (1194-1250) may have owed his nickname *Stupor Mundi* ('Wonder of the World') partly to the fact that he bathed often; the Knights Templar (*pages 80-81*) were not alone in making a religious virtue out of never bathing at all. Western medicine relied largely on herbs (which were sometimes surprisingly effective) and 'magical' theories (which were not). A medieval invalid probably valued his priest more than his doctor: the priest might open his way to Heaven; the doctor might simply hasten his journey! The Church hindered medical advance by forbidding dissection of dead bodies:

Leonardo da Vinci, it is said, paid large bribes to mortuary attendants and risked possible torture and death for blasphemy in order to carry out dissections for his great anatomical drawings.

Famines regularly swept the world, and starvation may have been an even greater killer than plague. The control of leprosy by isolation was one of Western medicine's few successes, but such diseases as bubonic plague, typhus, and malaria took dreadful toll. The Arabs, who translated the medical and other works of classical Greece long before they became generally known to Europe in the Renaissance (*pages 84-85*), and the Chinese, were far more advanced in medicine.

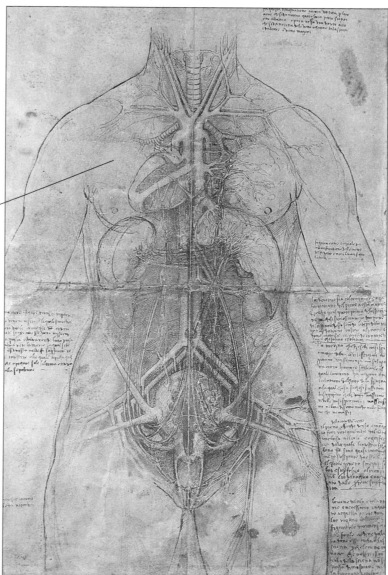

The great majority of medieval folk in Europe lived in small villages. They rarely traveled much beyond them. The feudal system decreed that a commoner owed service to his lord, who in return would protect him (there was, of course, no nationwide system of law enforcement other than rulers' armies). This tied peasants to their native fields. Most towns and cities were quite small. In 14th century England only about 10 per cent of the population lived in towns. In 1500, c.90 per cent of towns in Europe had 2,000 or fewer inhabitants. There were notable exceptions. Constantinople may have had c.300,000 inhabitants in the early Middle Ages. Italian city-states such as Venice, Florence, Milan, and Genoa all probably had around 100,000 citizens by the 14th century, far more than London or Paris at that time.

Most of the finest medieval cities lay outside Christendom. Peking probably had about 1,000,000 inhabitants in the 13th century, when Timbuktu, capital of the African empire of Mali (*pages 22-23*), may have excelled any European city in size and wealth. Culture and the quality of life in the great Muslim cities, such as Fez in North Africa and Córdoba in Moorish Spain, surpassed that of most of Europe. The world's oldest

The Duke of Berry sets out on a journey, c.1415. Other than noblemen, merchants, and soldiers, most medieval people seldom went far from home.

The courtyard of an ancient, mud walled mosque at Timbuktu (now Tombouctou, Mali). Unknown to Europeans, it was probably larger and richer than any of their cities in c.1200-1300.

surviving university was founded in Fez (in modern Morocco) in 859; Europe's oldest university, at Bologna, Italy, was not founded until 1088; England's Oxford University dates from c.1170. The Europeans who arrived in South America at the very end of the Middle Ages marveled at the great cities of the Incas and Aztecs (*pages 38-39*) – and at once proceeded to destroy them.

One of the greatest differences between medieval and modern people is that of religious faith. Although there were no doubt a fair proportion of medieval skeptics, they wisely kept their doubts to themselves. The medieval Roman Church was a great political as well as religious power, and those who differed openly from its teachings, like the Albigenses (Cathars) of southern France in the 13th century, were often hunted down by the civil authorities to be tortured and killed as 'heretics.'

The Pope authorized a military 'crusade' against the Albigenses, and it was as cruel and bloody as the long series of Crusader wars (*pages 56-57*)

Shearing sheep in June: the life of medieval agricultural workers was rarely as idyllic as it was painted by this artist in c.1515.

architecture shed glory alike on God and humanity.

The Middle Ages ended in an upsurge of intellectual and practical activity that was to shape the modern world. The 'new learning' of the 14th-15th centuries (*pages 84-85*) was spread by the new printing process (*pages 86-87*). Seeking to reconcile the teachings of Christ with those of the ancient Greek philosopher Plato, the thinker Pico della Mirandola (1463-94) concluded: 'Nothing can be found in the world more worthy of admiration than man.' This 'humanist' philosophy inspired thinkers, architects, painters and sculptors, writers and poets, scientists and explorers, to scale the heights of human creativity.

fought between Christians and Muslims for possession of the 'holy land' of Palestine. Jews were often savagely persecuted (*pages 44-45*) by Christians but (ironically, we may think, in view of 20th century events) found far more tolerance in the lands of Islam. It may be noted, however, that apart from Islamic-Christian conflicts the great 'wars of religion' post-dated the Middle Ages, occurring after the Protestant Reformation of the 16th century. The *Malleus Maleficarum* ('Hammer of the Witches') of the German Dominican monks Sprenger and Kramer appeared in 1486, but the savage 'witch hunts' it helped inspire were another post-Reformation phenomenon.

For all the Church's faults and abuses, it is probable that religious faith sustained and inspired most medieval people. They felt a strong personal relationship with God – beautifully expressed in the heart cry of a newly converted Irish prince (reported in a 10th century poem): 'O, how I should like to give a great ale-feast for the King of Kings!' The monks of the early medieval church preserved ancient learning that might have been lost in pagan invasions – although such supposed 'barbarians' as the Vikings (*pages 40-41*) enriched the West with their own vibrant culture. The medieval Church's patronage of art and

Almost all of the great art and architecture of the medieval West was inspired by the Christian religion – like the superb cathedral built in the 13th-16th centuries at Burgos, Spain.

Constantinople: Byzantine bulwark

After the Muslim conquest of Constantinople in 1453, graceful minarets were built to flank the former cathedral of St. Sophia.

In 330 Emperor Constantine I founded the capital of the Eastern Roman Empire on the site of the Greek city of Byzantium. Renamed Constantinople in his honor, it was often called by its earlier name; thus its possessions were the Byzantine Empire. When the Western Empire fell to barbarians in 476, Constantinople became sole capital of the Roman Empire. The first great Byzantine emperor, Justinian I (482-565), beat off Persian attacks, briefly regained the West, and laid the foundations of Byzantium's thousand year survival. He established a strong administrative and legal system, and his uncompromising championship of Christianity made his capital the center from which the Slav peoples were converted. By the 10th century Constantinople was the largest, finest city of Europe, its people still proudly calling themselves 'Romans.' The Byzantine Empire was the eastern bulwark of Western culture and religion: against it, invasions by Persians, Arabs, and Turks were broken; within it, classical learning was preserved and new arts fostered. But centuries of warfare weakened it; and after 1054, when a quarrel over papal authority caused the 'Schism' (split) between Western (Roman) and Eastern (Orthodox) churches, enmity grew between the Byzantine Empire and the West. The Crusades were launched in the 11th century to protect Constantinople from the Turks – but the city itself was sacked by the armies of the Fourth Crusade. The Byzantine Empire never recovered; its death blow was the capture of Constantinople by the Ottoman Turks (who renamed it Istanbul) in 1453.

This monumental head of Emperor Constantine I, founder of Constantinople and champion of Christianity, formed part of a huge statue erected in Rome in c.A.D. 313.

The dome of St. Sophia. The cathedral founded by Constantine became a mosque after 1453 and is now a museum.

Empress Theodora, wife of Justinian I, rose from humble origins to become the power behind her husband's throne.

A mosaic formed by carefully cut pieces of colored glass, marble, and other stones, portrays the splendor of the Byzantine court.

The last of the Romans

The last Roman emperor in the West, Romulus Augustus – called Augustulus ('Little Emperor') by the barbarian leaders who kept him in power – was deposed by Odoacer the Goth in 476. Odoacer in turn was overthrown and murdered in 493 by Theodoric the Great (455-526), king of the Ostrogoths, a Christian whose 35 year reign brought stability to an empire extending from eastern France to modern Yugoslavia. This period of relative peace ended when the Byzantine Emperor Justinian resolved to win back the West. His general Belisarius (505-565) first invaded North Africa, where his small army, supported by a powerful fleet of c.600 ships, beat far larger Vandal hordes. Belisarius has been called 'last of the Roman generals;' a better name would be 'first of the modern generals.' His armies little resembled the legions of Rome: most of his men were barbarian mercenaries; light cavalry rather than heavy infantry was his main strike force. In a 30 year career he won some 40 battles against odds, but by careful planning (he had a 'general staff' of executive and administrative officers), clever maneuver, and political manipulation (setting barbarian leaders against each other), rather than by confrontation. By c.555, mainly thanks to Belisarius, Justinian ruled both East and West. But the reunification of the Roman Empire was shortlived: by 568 Italy fell to the Lombards. Belisarius had also beaten off attacks from the east on Constantinople by the Persians and Bulgars (Huns). But after his death a new threat arose: inspired by the Prophet Muhammad, Muslim Arab peoples won North Africa and the Middle East, and by 717 were battering at the walls of Constantinople.

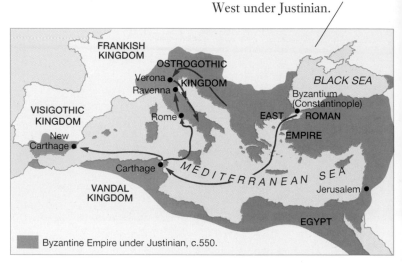

Arrows show the courses of the campaigns in which Byzantine general Belisarius regained the western territories of the old Roman Empire, briefly reuniting East and West under Justinian.

FRANKISH KINGDOM

OSTROGOTHIC KINGDOM

Verona
Ravenna

BLACK SEA

Byzantium (Constantinople)

VISIGOTHIC KINGDOM

Rome

EAST ROMAN EMPIRE

New Carthage

Carthage

MEDITERRANEAN SEA

Jerusalem

VANDAL KINGDOM

EGYPT

Byzantine Empire under Justinian, c.550.

Much of Constantinople's massive defenses – begun under Emperor Theodosius II in the 5th century and rebuilt over the centuries – survives in modern Istanbul. The fortress of Rumeli Hisari, seen here, dates from around 1200-1300.

Emperor Justinian, under whom the East and West Roman Empires were briefly reunited, is shown on an ivory carving of the 6th century.

Light cavalry were the mainstay of the armies of Belisarius.

❏ In 562 Justinian (above) accused Belisarius of conspiracy and imprisoned him. A long lasting legend (some books still repeat it as truth) is that the great general ended his life as a blind beggar, pleading 'Give an *obolus* [small coin] to Belisarius.' In fact, he was restored to favor, dying wealthy and respected in 565, the same year as Justinian.

❏ Barbarian invaders spread at least one major benefit throughout the West. Nomadic horsemen habitually wore leg wrappings to prevent chafing of their lower limbs – and with their conquests the useful garments we call pants or trousers ousted the dignified but impractical Roman toga.

❏ Lombards from the Danube area overran north Italy after Belisarius's departure. In 572 their leader Alboin defeated a rival people, the Gepids, and had their king's skull made into a cup. He forcibly married the dead king's daughter. At the marriage feast he passed the skull-cup to her and demanded she 'drink with her father.' She obeyed – but cleverly poisoned the cup before passing it back. Alboin died still laughing at his own sick joke.

Monks and missionaries

By the 6th century the conquests made by pagan, barbarian peoples faced the Roman popes with the problem of 'reconverting' Western Europe. The medium through which Pope Gregory I the Great (c.540-604) and others worked to this end was the monastic movement. Monasticism originated with the ascetics (early Christian hermits) of the Middle East, who (like St. Simeon Stylites who lived 30 years on the top of a tall pillar) sometimes carried self-denial to odd extremes. An Italian monk, St. Benedict of Nursia (c.480-550), transformed asceticism into a disciplined, useful movement. His 'Benedictine Rule' established the two great principles of monastic life: '*Ora et labora*' ('prayer and work'). Monks lived by a strict timetable of prayer, labor (to make their communities self-supporting), and study. In the centuries following the fall of the Roman Empire, the monks' care for books and learning, especially their copying of ancient documents, was chiefly responsible for preserving Western culture. From the monasteries, missionaries went forth among the pagans. St. Patrick (d.c.463), probably born in Wales, was kidnaped by sea raiders, spent his youth as a slave in pagan Ireland, escaped to a French monastery, and in c.432 returned to Ireland as a missionary. From newly-Christian Ireland, where Western monasticism was first firmly established, St. Columba (521-97) went to convert Scotland and northern England, while St. Columban (543-615) traveled as far as what is now Switzerland. Pope Gregory's mission to England in 596 was led by St. Augustine (Austin) of Canterbury (d.604), who is said to have baptized 10,000 Anglo-Saxons in one day. But not until the 9th century was Western Europe predominantly Christian.

The lovely 'Ardagh Chalice,' a silver bowl with gold filigree and enamel decoration, was made for an Irish monastery around the 8th century.

'Enclosed' monks never left their monasteries; others, as seen here, went out into the world.

'Cleanliness is next to godliness' – so these monks have taken off their black robes and are apparently happy at the prospect of taking a bath in a little brook.

A masterpiece of British Christian art, the *Lindisfarne Gospels* were written out by the monks of Lindisfarne Abbey, Northumbria, in c.696-98, and dedicated to their former Prior, St. Cuthbert (634-87).

A celestial globe and other objects symbolizing learning and holiness furnish the study of St. Augustine (Austin) in a 15th century painting.

Beside the saint, the artist Sandro Botticelli (1444-1510) shows the miter (headdress) he wore as an Archbishop.

❏ St. Columba was a 'prince' of the powerful Ui Niall (O'Neill) family of Ireland. He made good use of this in his missionary work. He is said to have told Pictish (Scottish) chiefs: 'I am an O'Neill. Accept Christ – or I will bring my clansmen from Ireland and massacre the lot of you!' Bede (d.735) wrote that Columba saved one of his monks from a 'savage water beast' in the Ness River by cowing it with the sign of the Cross. This was the first record of the 'Loch Ness Monster.'

❏ One of the toughest monastic disciplines was imposed by St. Columban. He was expelled from France, where he founded three monasteries, when other churchmen complained of his severity. Under his rule a monk who sang out of tune or forgot to say 'Amen' got six lashes with a scourge; one who whittled a table with his knife got ten strokes.

❏ One of the greatest early English monasteries was Whitby, Yorkshire, where St. Hilda (616-80) was the patroness of Caedmon, said to be the first man to use the English language (rather than Latin) for Christian poetry. Tradition says Caedmon was a peasant monk, so unscholarly that he was given the job of cowherd. While watching his flocks, a vision inspired him to compose a hymn of the Creation: the first datable English poem.

Empires in Africa

It was once believed that Africa south of the Sahara was not 'civilized' until after the arrival of Europeans in the late 15th century. In fact, prosperous, well organized states existed there throughout the Middle Ages. Between the 8th and 17th centuries, three African Muslim empires dominated the Niger River area of West Africa. By c.800, Ghana (not the modern state, which is farther south) was known to the Arabs of North Africa as the 'land of gold.' Their camel caravans took salt, weapons, and manufactured goods south across the Sahara, and returned with gold, ivory, and slaves. By the 13th century, when the empire of Mali supplanted Ghana, West African mines produced some two-thirds of the world's gold supply. Under Kankan (Emperor) Mansa Musa (ruled 1307-37), Mali's capital, Timbuktu, became a center of Islamic learning. Mali's successor, the Songhay Empire, perhaps founded as early as the 7th century, was conquered by Moroccan Arabs in 1591, but farther south, in what is now Nigeria, the kingdom of Benin survived until modern times. Founded in the 13th century, Benin prospered on trade in textiles, metalwork, ivory, spices, and (especially with the arrival of Portuguese traders from 1472) slaves. Like the nearby state of Ife, Benin is famed for artworks in bronze, brass, and ivory. Much farther south, Zimbabwe flourished from the 10th century, exporting gold and copper through the Arab traders of Mozambique. Dating from the 10th-15th centuries, the stone-built city of Great Zimbabwe, estimated to have housed 20,000 people (as many as earlier medieval London), is the greatest ancient monument to any purely African civilization.

The granite walls of Great Zimbabwe were built by the ancestors of the Shona people of the modern African state.

Ghana, Mali, and Songhay prospered on trans-Saharan trade with North African Arabs – who then took over the black empires. In the south, Zimbabwe gave way to the black Rozvi Empire (Monomatapa) after 1480.

Metal sculptures, like this brass figure of a court musician dating from the 16th-17th century, were made to beautify the courts of the kings of Benin.

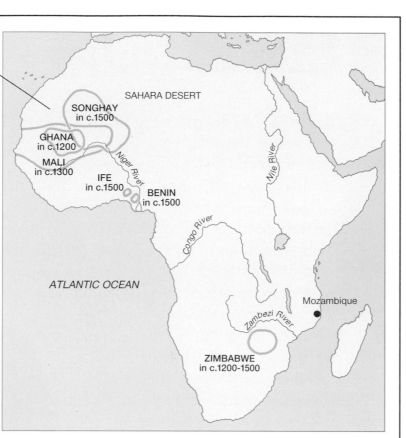

SAHARA DESERT

SONGHAY
in c.1500

GHANA
in c.1200

MALI
in c.1300

IFE
in c.1500

BENIN
in c.1500

Niger River

Nile River

Congo River

ATLANTIC OCEAN

Mozambique

Zambezi River

ZIMBABWE
in c.1200-1500

Timbuktu (the modern Tombouctou, Mali), site of this old adobe mosque, was the capital of two great medieval Muslim empires.

Fine artworks like this bronze head were made in Ife (Nigeria) from the 12th century.

❑ In 1324 Mansa Musa of Mali made the *haj* (Muslim pilgrimage) to Mecca (now in Saudi Arabia). He traveled with a 15,000 strong cavalry escort and 100 camels loaded with gold. The arrival of so much bullion threw the Middle East's money markets into turmoil. Timbuktu, his capital (and later that of the Songhay rulers), became legendary for its wealth and splendor throughout the medieval world – but no European reached it until the 19th century.

❑ The art of Benin was little known in Europe until the early 20th century. The massacre in 1897 of a British force sent to suppress the slave trade and rituals involving human sacrifice provoked reprisals in which Benin City was razed. Vast quantities of artworks were looted for the European 'curio' market – and soon inspired many great modern painters and sculptors.

❑ Until very recently, many Europeans (especially white colonists in Africa) refused to believe that Great Zimbabwe was the work of black Africans untouched by the white races' influence. They theorized that the mighty stone structures were built by the biblical Queen of Sheba (Zimbabwe's gold workings were identified with 'King Solomon's Mines'), by a 'lost' Roman legion, by a 'lost tribe of Israel,' or by 'Egyptian' settlers from the ancient Nubian empire of Kush-Meroë.

The golden age of India

The magnificent Hindu temples at Khajuraho date from the 11th century, when Muslims dominated northern India.

For long after Alexander the Great's invasion in the 4th century B.C., India was dominated by Greek-influenced peoples from north Asia. In c.A.D. 320 a native dynasty was founded by a Hindu chief who, by clever diplomacy as much as force, built an empire centering on Pataliputra (Patna) in the Ganges basin. He took the name of an emperor of Alexander's time, Chandragupta, and all his successors took names ending '-gupta' ('protector'). Under two strong, long-lived rulers, Samudragupta (reigned 330-75) and Chandragupta II (reigned 375-415), the Gupta empire embraced much of north, central, and east India. This period of prosperity and religious tolerance has been called India's golden age. Hindu and Buddhist culture flourished: Sanskrit literature reached its peak in the work of the poet and dramatist Kalidasa (c.388-455); magnificent stone temples were raised. But in the late 500s the Gupta realm was destroyed by White Huns from central Asia. Muslim invasion from Afghanistan followed; by the 13th century north India was ruled from Delhi by Muslim sultans. From south India, the Pallava dynasty, established c.350 with its capital at Kanchipuram near Madras, spread Hinduism into Southeast Asia. Its greatest monuments are the temples at Mahabalipuram, built in 625-74. After c.880 the Pallavas gave way to the Chola dynasty. These Tamil Hindus invaded Ceylon (Sri Lanka) in 1018, and in 1021 sent a seaborne expeditionary force as far as Sumatra. Rival states brought down their farflung trading empire in the late 13th century. By the time of the Mogul (Mongol) invasion of the later Middle Ages, most of India had fragmented into small, warring states.

A gold coin struck during the reign of Chandragupta II (375-415) shows the ruler on horseback, perhaps reflecting his success in extending his empire by conquest.

Shiva (the 'Benign One') is often depicted with four arms.

Parvati, consort of Shiva, is shown in her benevolent aspect in an 11th century sculpture of the Chola period.

Shiva is one of three gods – the others are Brahma and Vishnu – of the Hindu trinity.

This sandstone *vimana* (shrine) dedicated to the Hindu deity Shiva is one of 30 Hindu and Jain temples at Khajuraho.

The influence of the religious architecture of Gupta India, where both Hindu and Buddhist cultures flourished, is seen in the huge Buddhist temple complex at Borobodur, Java, built in c.750-850.

FACT FILE

❏ A classic of Sanskrit literature has been a modern bestseller in the West: the *Kama Sutra*, a detailed guide to sexual techniques. It is ascribed to the 5th century scholar Vatsayana Mallagana of Benares (Varanasi). He stressed that sexuality was a vital part of the 'wholeness' essential to a person's true and complete understanding of spiritual matters.

❏ An eyewitness account of Gupta India is preserved in the memoirs of a Chinese Buddhist monk, Fu-Hsien, who spent 15 years there in 399-414. Although he complained that the mountains along the northern border 'shelter dragons that spit out poison,' he is considered a reliable witness. Another monk, Hsuan-Tsang, traveled India in 629-45. It is said he returned to China with so many Buddhist relics that he needed a chariot so big that it was drawn by 20 horses in which to carry them.

❏ India was almost totally unknown to medieval Westerners. King Alfred the Great of England (849-99) sent explorers to seek the tomb of the Apostle Thomas, whom legend said had carried the word of Jesus to India. Alfred's own geographical writings identify India only as 'the land across the Don River' (i.e., somewhere beyond west central Russia), so it is no surprise that nothing more was heard of the intrepid Anglo-Saxon adventurers.

Islam: a faith in arms

Muezzins (religious officials) have called Muslims to prayer from the summits of Egyptian mosques since the 7th century, when Egypt was taken from the Byzantine Empire by the warriors of the new Islamic faith.

This spiral minaret rises over the Ibn Tulun Mosque, Cairo, erected in 876-79. In the 10th century the Fatimid dynasty made Cairo (al-Qahira) capital of Egypt.

The Prophet Muhammad (c.570-632) perhaps has had a greater impact on the world than any other medieval man. He was born in Mecca (now in Saudi Arabia) in c.570, and at the age of 40 was a prosperous merchant with little interest in religion. Then, in a vision, the Angel Gabriel commanded him to preach the one god, Allah. The citizens of Mecca, who profited from pilgrims to the Kabah ('cube,' a small, square temple, housing a wonder-working black stone, probably a meteorite), resented his attacks on their paganism, and the Prophet and his followers were forced to migrate to Medina. Here Muhammad received more divine revelations that he set down in the *Koran*, holy book of Islam ('Submission [to the will of Allah]'). By the time of his death, Muslims ('those who submit') dominated much of Arabia. From the first, social and economic factors dictated that Islam must be a dynamic, militant faith – and under the caliphs ('successors'), its leaders after Muhammad, its expansion was amazingly swift. By 700 Muslim warriors (called Saracens or Moors by Europeans) had taken Syria, Palestine, Iraq, and Iran, and were advancing through North Africa. Within 100 years of Muhammad's death, Islam controlled about half the western world, from north India to Spain. The year 732 saw the invasion of France: only defeat at Tours (Poitiers), where the Frankish leader Charles Martel ('the Hammer') smashed a Saracen host, saved the European heartland from an Islamic flood. Although rivalry between Muslim leaders prevented further Arab efforts at conquest on this scale, Saracen raiders – who in 846 sacked Rome – were as much feared in southern Europe as their Viking contemporaries were to the north.

Written in an ancient form of Arabic script, this copy of the *Koran* (*Qu'ran*), holy book of Islam, dates from the 8th century. The first definitive *Koran* was produced by Zayd ibn Thabit in 651.

Enclosed in the Great Mosque (Haram) at Mecca, the stone and marble shrine called the Kabah, seen here in a 15th century manuscript, is Islam's holiest place.

Like these worshipers, all Muslims are supposed to make a pilgrimage (*haj*) to Mecca, Muhammad's birthplace.

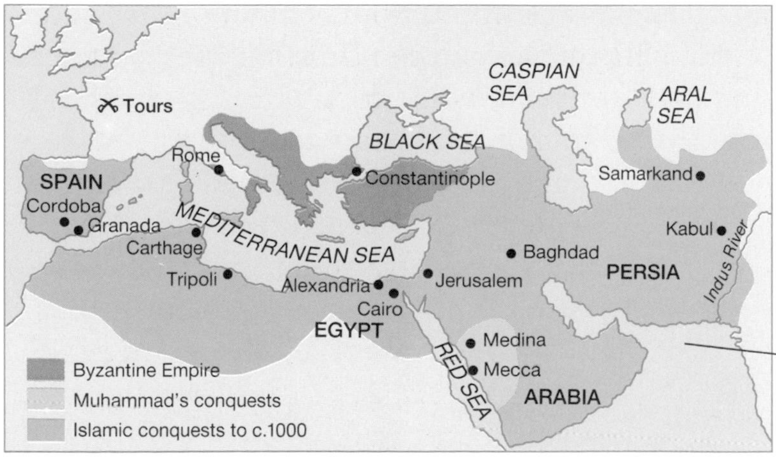

CASPIAN SEA
ARAL SEA
Tours
BLACK SEA
Rome
SPAIN
Constantinople
Samarkand
Cordoba
Granada
MEDITERRANEAN SEA
Kabul
Carthage
Baghdad
Indus River
Tripoli
Alexandria
Jerusalem
PERSIA
Cairo
EGYPT
Medina
RED SEA
Mecca
ARABIA
Byzantine Empire
Muhammad's conquests
Islamic conquests to c.1000

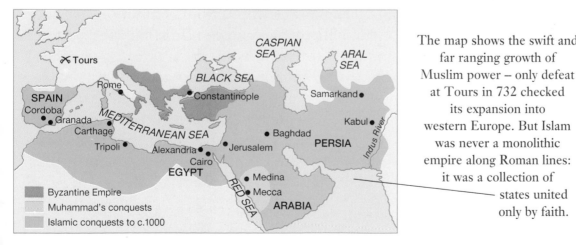

The map shows the swift and far ranging growth of Muslim power – only defeat at Tours in 732 checked its expansion into western Europe. But Islam was never a monolithic empire along Roman lines: it was a collection of states united only by faith.

FACT FILE

❑ The *Hegira* (journey) of Muhammad and his followers from Mecca to Medina in 622 marks the start of the Islamic calendar, in which years are designated 'A.H.' In 630 Muhammad returned in triumph to Mecca and purified the Kabah, destroying all its pagan images. Today, the Kabah, covered for most of the year by the Kiswa (a cloth of black brocade embroidered with verses from the *Koran*) is an Islamic shrine.

❑ The Muslim temple called the Dome of the Rock (above), one of the glories of Jerusalem, was built in 685-705, soon after the Arabs occupied the holy city. It is a reminder that medieval Muslim culture in many ways equaled that of Christian Europe – and in some fields, such as medicine, was superior.

❑ Arab civilization reached its height under the Abbasid caliphate of Baghdad (750-1258). The best remembered Abbasid ruler – through the collection of Arab folk tales known as 'The Thousand and One Nights,' or 'Arabian Nights' – is Caliph Harun al-Rashid (763-809).

Charlemagne: maker of the Middle Ages

'Hail Charles Augustus . . . great and peace-bringing Emperor of the Romans!' This salute rang through St. Peter's, Rome, on Christmas Day, 800, as Pope Leo III crowned King Charles of the Franks (c.742-814) (Charles the Great; Charlemagne) as Emperor of the West. A 'Roman' emperor again ruled much of the old Roman Empire. Charlemagne's greatness lay not in his revival of ancient glories, but in his impact on centuries to come. Heroic war leader, shrewd statesman, and patron of art and learning, he, more than any other ruler, set a pattern for the Middle Ages. Grandson of Charles Martel, who had halted the Moors' invasion of Europe, Charlemagne became leader of the Franks (Germanic peoples of France, Belgium, and the Lower Rhine) in 771. In the course of conquering the pagan Saxon tribes (772-81), bringing Bavaria and Lombardy (north Italy) under his control, and destroying the Avar (Hunnish) state in Hungary, he developed the model medieval army: well disciplined, uniformly equipped foot soldiers – and a strike force of armored horsemen (the first 'knights'). The 'feudal system,' based on a military nobility owing duty to a monarch, who in turn guaranteed their holding of large estates and their local rule over common people, largely evolved from Charlemagne's military organization and imposition of centralized authority. His capital at Aachen (Aix-la-Chapelle) was the cultural center of Europe; the 'Carolingian renaissance' of his time marked the first great revival of western culture. His empire was divided into separate kingdoms by squabbling successors, but he had set a standard that the greatest rulers of the later Middle Ages would strive to reach.

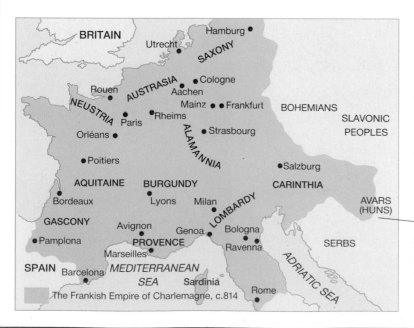

The Frankish Empire of Charlemagne, c.814

Charlemagne's military campaigns added Saxony, Lombardy, and other eastern territories to the Frankish Empire (compare with map on *page 46*) – but he was unable to extend his rule far into Islamic Spain.

A coronet preserved at Monza Cathedral, north Italy: said to be the 'iron crown' of Charlemagne.

At Aachen (Aix-la-Chapelle), now in Germany, center of his empire, Charlemagne built a magnificent cathedral and royal chapel (rebuilt in the 10th century).

A French chronicle of the 14th century shows Charlemagne receiving news of a victory over the Muslims of Spain, where he was able to set up a Christian 'march' (zone) along the northern border.

❏ Charlemagne's parents were Pepin 'the Short' and Berthe *au grand pied* ('Bigfoot Bertha;' but the name may mean that she had long, narrow feet – then considered a mark of beauty). Charlemagne himself was a giant, some 6ft 4in (1.93m) tall at a time when the average man's height was c.5ft 6in (1.67m), but is said to have had a high, squeaky voice.

❏ Charlemagne's spiritual health was looked after at the great Benedictine monastery of Saint-Riquier, northern France. There, 12 bishops and 400 clergy, working a 24 hour, three shift day at 30 altars, prayed continually for the Emperor, aided by the relics of 56 martyrs, 14 virgins, and 48 other holy saints.

❏ Charlemagne and his 'knights' ranked with King Arthur as the heroes of later medieval legends. Ironically, the most famous of these, the *Chanson de Roland*, records one of his few setbacks: the defeat at Roncesvalles in the Pyrenees in 778 of his expedition into Islamic Spain.

❏ Charlemagne feared that if his daughters married, their sons might fight for his kingdom. It is said that he encouraged them to have love affairs rather than marry, and undertook to make generous settlements on their children – so long as these were illegitimate and could have no claim to the throne.

The dawn of England

The 'Sutton Hoo Treasure' was found in a ship burial mound, probably that of King Raedwald (d.624) of East Anglia.

Soon after Rome withdrew from Britain in the early 5th century, Anglo-Saxon war bands from Germany, Frisia (Holland), and Jutland (Denmark) arrived. Some came by invitation, as mercenaries hired to hold off Celtic raiders in the north, others as invaders. Beginning as a medley of Germanic tribes – Angles, Saxons, Jutes, Frisians, Franks – the Anglo-Saxons gradually became one nation. During some 150 years' occupation of the land they renamed England, they became the English. In many ways they had more in common with native Britons than had the earlier Roman conquerors. Rome had aimed to unite 'Britannia' into a single province: the Anglo-Saxons, like the Britons, preferred to divide it into small tribal kingdoms. Heroic warriors, pagan followers of the war god Woden (equivalent to the Norse Odin), they were also masters of metalwork, who made not only weapons but also fine jewelry, and skilfull poets, whose complex works were not written down but preserved by word of mouth. The arrival of Christianity introduced them to a wider culture. From 596 missionaries led by St. Augustine brought to England not only Christianity but also the learning of Greece and Rome. The Anglo-Saxons learned to read and write, and acquired new creative skills. They began to build stone churches and produce magnificent illuminated manuscripts. They also began to turn toward a more centralized social organization. From the early 7th century there arose a succession of dominant kingdoms: first Northumbria, then Mercia, and at last Wessex, under the forerunners of King Alfred the Great.

Superb examples of Anglo-Saxon metalwork unearthed at Sutton Hoo, Suffolk, included this gold clasp, decorated with inlaid garnets and pieces of colored glass.

This impressive iron helmet incorporating the face mask of a mustached warrior, and originally decorated with bronze reliefs of battle scenes, is thought to have been made by Swedish craftsmen.

Many of the peoples who made up the Anglo-Saxon race originally came to Britain as invaders. An 11th century artist shows (in costume of his own time) Britons opposing a 'barbarian' raid.

The shields of the dead and wounded are kite shaped – of 11th century Norman type.

Map shows English kingdoms of the 7th-9th centuries: Northumbria, Mercia, Wessex were in turn dominant. Alfred of Wessex (*pages 32-33*) drove Danish invaders out of the south-west into the 'Danelaw' to the north and east.

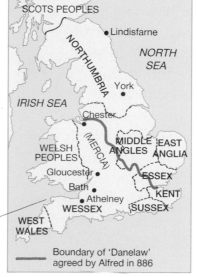

SCOTS PEOPLES
NORTHUMBRIA
Lindisfarne
NORTH SEA
IRISH SEA
York
Chester
(MERCIA)
MIDDLE ANGLES
EAST ANGLIA
WELSH PEOPLES
Gloucester
ESSEX
Bath
KENT
Athelney
WESSEX
SUSSEX
WEST WALES

Boundary of 'Danelaw' agreed by Alfred in 886

❏ The name 'England' comes from the people called Angles (Old English *Engle*; Latin *Angli*). It did not replace the country's older names, Albion and Britannia, until the 11th century, when '*Englaland*' ('land of the Angles') and '*Angelcynn*' ('the Angle nation') came into regular use.

❏ Early chronicles recording battles between native British and Anglo-Saxons describe a great British victory in c.500 at Mons Badonicus (Mount Badon), which inhibited invaders for some 50 years. Most modern scholars believe there was a battle of Badon, although the site has never been identified; some accept the tradition that the British were led there by the legendary King Arthur (below).

❏ The pagan gods of the Anglo-Saxons left their mark on our everyday vocabulary. Tuesday, Wednesday, Thursday, and Friday are named in honor of war god Tiw, chief god Woden, thunder-god Thunor, and fertility goddess Frig.

Alfred the Great: 'England's darling'

Anglo-Saxon chroniclers say that 'fiery dragons' (comets) in the sky, storms, and famine heralded the first Danish raid on England in 793. The fearful omens were right: Danish warbands terrorized the land, and after 865 smash-and-grab raids gave way to invasion and occupation. The king of Kent tried to buy off the Danes – but they took his money, then his kingdom, then seized Northumbria and Mercia. In 870 they turned to Wessex, where an English champion emerged: King Alfred (reigned 871-891). Although a scholar (then rare; England was being driven back to barbarism) and in poor health, Alfred was a great military leader and strategist. In his first year as king he fought nine battles, driving the Danes to seek prey elsewhere. In 876 they returned under King Guthrum. Alfred defeated him, but next year Guthrum succeeded with a surprise attack and in 878 drove Alfred back to his base at Athelney. In apparent defeat, Alfred swiftly rallied men from all over Wessex, won a decisive victory, and drove out the Danes.

A stylized portrait of Alfred the Great, King of Wessex (southern England), is seen on an Anglo-Saxon silver penny struck during his reign, in around 885.

Hoping to encourage peaceful settlement, he gave them land to the north and east: the 'Danelaw.' It was not only military skill that earned Alfred the title 'the Great' and led to the nickname 'England's darling.' A symbol of resistance for all England, he gave a new meaning to the word 'king,' and in effect founded the English monarchy. He strengthened the country by raising forts, building a fleet, reorganizing the army, and establishing a national code of law; all of which would aid his successors. Determined to restore learning, he founded schools (traditionally including University College, Oxford), and commissioned English translations of Latin texts.

The 'White Horse' of Westbury, Wiltshire: such figures cut into southern English chalk hills are said to mark Alfred's victories over Danish invaders.

Seal ring of King Aethelwulf (d.858) of Wessex, who defeated Danish invaders in 850. His four sons succeeded in turn: Alfred was youngest.

Wantage, Alfred's birthplace, honors the great ruler with a 19th century statue. It shows a tough war leader; in fact, Alfred was in chronic ill health for almost all of his life.

Found near Athelney, the 'Alfred Jewel' has a portrait in cloisonné enamel set in rock crystal of a ruler with two scepters: perhaps a portrait of Alfred himself.

The gold base of the jewel is in the shape of a boar's head. The frame bears an inscription in Anglo-Saxon, translating as: 'Alfred ordered me to be made.'

The scroll held by Alfred (with a marker much resembling the 'Alfred Jewel') commemorates his great love of learning.

❏ As a child, Alfred twice visited Rome – whose glories may have inspired his lifelong devotion to learning. His works include a translation of a 4th century history of the world by the monk Orosius, to which Alfred added notes on European history and geography – including interviews with travelers to his court. Among these were Ohthere, a Norwegian from the Arctic lands, and Wulfstan, a Dane, both of whom described great sea voyages exploring unknown territory (and at the same time seeking wealth from fur trapping, sealing, and whaling) in the Far North and around the Baltic Sea.

❏ It is odd that for all his greatness, Alfred should be remembered for 'burning the cakes.' Tradition says that during a time of defeat he took refuge in a cowherd's hut. Not knowing him, the cowherd's wife set him to tend her baking, but his mind was on campaigns, not cakes. She found the whole batch burned and gave him a thorough scolding. The story, though repeated for centuries, is almost certainly untrue.

❏ Alfred's great-great-grandson, King Ethelred of England (968-1016), is popularly known to history as 'the Unready.' In fact his nickname 'Unraed' really means 'Ill-Advised': it is a pun on his name of Ethelred, which means 'noble counsel' or 'good advice.'

Cambodian 'kings of the mountain'

In 1860 a French traveler discovered in the Cambodian jungle 'temples grander than anything left by Greece and Rome.' These were the monuments of the 'kings of the mountain,' rulers of the Khmer Empire. In the 1st century A.D. Indonesian settlers established a Hindu kingdom, Funan, in the Mekong River valley. By the 6th century native Khmer Buddhists dominated, but the monarchs remained Hindus. In 802 Jayavarman II founded a new capital on the shore of Lake Tonle Sap. Here, at Angkor, Khmer emperors established a succession of capitals on a 40sq mi (104sq km) site. The major work of each emperor was to construct a temple to be his shrine, and to this end thousands of his subjects were pressed into forced labor. Greatest of the monuments is the temple of Angkor Wat, built for Suryavarman II in 1113-50. At its center, the emperor's pyramidal shrine represents the Himalayan peak of Mount Meru, sacred to Hindus; it stands within three enclosures, the outer one measuring 1,510 x 1,245yd (1,380 x 1,150m). Its rich carvings give a comprehensive picture of Khmer life, from the labors of peasants to the religious ceremonies of the court – and the bloody wars fought with its neighbors. At its height, under Jayavarman VII (1181-c.1220), builder of Angkor Thom, a moated city c.1.75mi (2.8km) square, the Khmer empire extended over modern Cambodia, Laos, and southern Vietnam. But its people wearied of toil for the glory of god-emperors, and the vast irrigation works that sustained Angkor's rice economy fell into disrepair. In c.1430, the advance of the Thai Empire from the west drove the Khmer capital from Angkor to Phnom Penh.

A huge stone face looks down from the Gate of the Dead, one of four main entrances to the 12th century temple-city of Angkor Thom.

Centuries of tropical rains have eroded the ancient stones.

A paved causeway across a *baray* (reservoir) leads to the central temple at Angkor Wat. The highest tower, shrine of Emperor Suryavarman II, represents the holy peak of Mount Meru.

Khmer spearmen march out to battle: a scene from the superb bas-reliefs on the Bayon, the Buddhist temple at the heart of Angkor Thom.

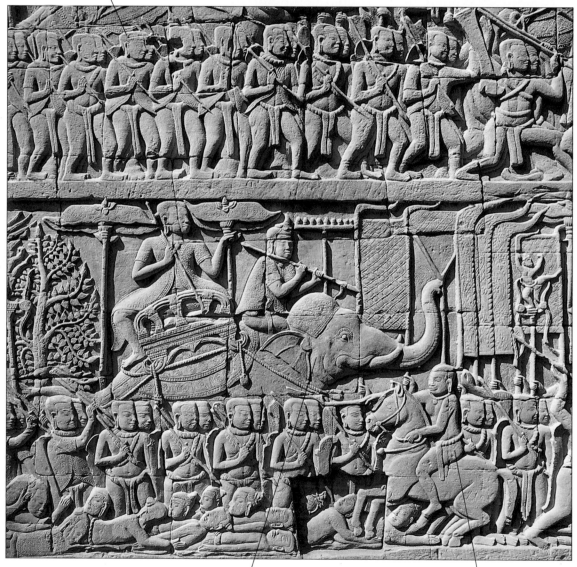

A Khmer leader, perhaps Jayavarman VII, whose victories over the Champa people of Vietnam the carvings commemorate, rides on an elephant.

Jayavarman's conquest of the Champa kingdom in 1190 avenged Champa's capture and sacking of Angkor in 1177.

Japan's warriors and warlords

By the 5th century A.D. Japan's heartland on the Inland Sea was ruled by the Yamato clan. Emperors encouraged the spread of Chinese sciences, arts, and Confucian and Buddhist beliefs, and by the early 8th century had established a Chinese-style bureaucratic government with its capital at Nara. After the capital moved to Heian (Kyoto) in 794 the Fujiwara clan seized control and the emperors became ceremonial figureheads. Central government weakened, and *daimyo* (clan chief) warlords carved out huge domains with *samurai* armies. The Japanese warrior class evolved from the mounted archers who guarded emperors and nobles from the 4th century. By c.1000 they were called *samurai* ('serving men'), and usually fought on foot, with sword or *naginata* (pole ax); firearms did not reach Japan until the 16th century. By the 12th century the *samurai* were ruled by *bushido* ('way of the warrior'), a Zen Buddhist code stressing that a *samurai* must be always ready to sacrifice his life for emperor, *daimyo*, or his own honor. He must not consider his own comfort or safety and, facing defeat, must kill himself rather than surrender. A clan war in 1160 brought down the Fujiwara, and in 1192 Minamoto Yoritomo (1147-99) took power as the first *shogun* ('great general'), military overlord of Japan, ruling from Kamakura in the name of the emperor. The rule of the *shogun* would last until the 19th century. Under the Kamakura shogunate, invasions by Mongols under Kublai Khan were repulsed in 1274 and 1281. In 1338 the Ashikaga clan took the shogunate. Their rule saw long periods of civil war and, in the later 1500s, the first penetration of Japan by Europeans.

Kyoto (its ancient name was Heian-kyo: 'place of tranquillity'), site of this graceful temple, became Japan's capital in 794.

It was said that 'the sword is the soul of the *samurai*,' and the long-bladed, slashing sword (*katana*) is the weapon associated with Japan's warriors – although they were originally archers.

Samurai stories were (and still are) a major feature of Japanese popular culture. This print of c.1800 shows *kabuki* (non-classical theater) actors as *samurai*.

Haniwa, hollow pottery figures like this warrior, were made in the Yamato era (3rd-7th centuries) as tomb ornaments.

Lovingly restored, this temple of the Heian period keeps its ancient elegance.

'After victory, tighten your helmet strings,' was one of the mottos of the *samurai*, ever ready for battle.

O yoroi ('great armor') of the late medieval Ashikaga period: an exact replica presented by Japan's last *shogun* to Britain's Queen Victoria in 1860.

Fine boots complete the ensemble: such armor was rarely worn in battle.

FACT FILE

❏ The words of Japan's national anthem, the *Kimigayo*, date from the 9th century. As well as being the world's oldest anthem, it is one of the shortest – only four lines long.

❏ *Samurai*, comprising c.5 per cent of the population of medieval Japan, were the only class allowed to bear arms. Some martial arts now associated with *samurai*, like *aikido* (a type of judo) and *jodo* (fighting with a staff), were in fact developed by unarmed peasants for protection against tyrannical *samurai*.

❏ A *samurai* retained his caste only as long as he served a *daimyo*. If he had no *daimyo* he became a *ronin*, a mercenary warrior. Some *ronin* became *ninja*: black-clad, spies and assassins.

❏ The two swords (*daisho*) of the *samurai* were the *katana* (below), a long sword with a slightly curved blade and a two-handed hilt, and the shorter *wakisashi*. The latter was both a close-quarter weapon and, if defeat seemed inevitable, the blade with which its owner committed *seppuku* (ceremonial suicide). Both were carried in a waist belt, always with blades uppermost so that a killing stroke could be delivered immediately the sword cleared the scabbard.

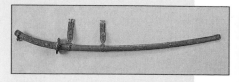

Victims of the 'Feathered Serpent'

The flourishing medieval cultures of Mesoamerica (modern Mexico, Belize, Guatemala, Honduras, and El Salvador) were ruled by priest-kings. Their religion centered on the Sun, worshiped in pyramid-temples. A common cult was that of Quetzalcoatl ('Feathered Serpent'), an exiled god who would one day return as a 'savior.' The first great medieval Mesoamerican culture, the city-state of Teotihuacán, central Mexico, reached its height in c.600-700. It was overthrown by the warlike Toltecs, who established a capital at Tula. From c.1000 they expanded into Yucatán, fuzing with the older Mayan culture to produce, at Chichén Itzá, a Maya-Toltec city centering on the Cenote ('Well of Sacrifice'), into which offerings of treasure and human sacrifices were thrown. The Toltecs gave way to the Aztecs, who founded their capital at Tenochtitlán (modern Mexico City) in c.1320. They believed the Sun god, Huitzilopochtli, needed human hearts to help him combat the darkness, and sacrificed up to 50,000 persons each year. Farther south, the Incas of Peru flourished at same time. In c.1420-1520 their empire extended over c.280,000sq mi (725,000sq km), from Ecuador to Chile. This vast area was connected by more than 10,000mi (16,000km) of paved highway. The first Spaniards to arrive in the 'New World,' from c.1500, described the Aztec capital as 'more splendid than Rome,' and marveled too at the works of the Incas. Yet within decades they destroyed both cultures. The Aztecs, overawed by the Spaniards' horses and weapons, made little effective resistance – perhaps because they identified the invaders with the long-awaited 'savior' Quetzalcoatl.

A mosaic of colored and semi-precious stones forms a grotesque Mixtec mask.

The mask may represent Tezcatlipoca, an Aztec sun god also worshiped by the Mixtecs who flourished in the Oaxaca region of Mexico from around A.D. 700.

Steep flights of steps lead to the place of sacrifice atop a Mayan pyramid temple.

Toltec-Maya remains at Chichén Itzá date from the 10th-12th centuries. The city was dedicated to Kukulcan (Quetzalcoatl).

An ancient Mesoamerican culture, existing from around 1200 B.C., was that of the Olmecs of Mexico's gulf coast, makers of these giants.

The huge figures may have supported a temple. Olmec remains are thought to have influenced the medieval cultures of the Maya, Toltecs, and Aztecs.

❏ Cholula (Cholula de Rivadabia, Mexico) was a sacred site for both Toltecs and Aztecs. Its Teocali de Cholula, built in c.200-500 to honor Quetzalcoatl, is the world's largest pyramid, rising to 177ft (54m) from a base c.45 acres (18ha) in area. In 1519 the Spanish conqueror Cortez massacred the city's people and ordered a Christian church built atop the great pyramid.

❏ Tlachtli, sacred ball game of the Aztecs, was a kind of basketball. A goal scoring player was entitled to claim the clothing of spectators as a reward (probably not the origin of the expression 'to lose one's shirt' on a game!). Similar religious games were played by other Mesoamerican peoples. The Toltec ball court at Chichén Itzá is 270ft (83m) long; its carved decoration includes a scene apparently showing the captain of a losing team being sacrificed to the nation's gods.

❏ In spite of their magnificent highways, the Incas had no wheeled vehicles: messages were carried by runners, goods by porters or llamas. Nor did they develop the art of writing. They kept records on *quipus*: hanks of cords of different color and thickness, tied with a system of coded knots. It is believed that *chasquis* (running messengers) organized on a relay system at c.2mi (3.2km) intervals along the highways could carry messages as much as 150mi (240km) in one day.

Viking sea rovers

'From the fury of the Northmen, O Lord, deliver us!' For more than two centuries, from c.800, that prayer was offered up all over Europe, as the dragon-prowed longships of the Vikings ('Northmen' from Denmark, Norway, and Sweden) terrorized many nations. But these master seafarers were not just pirates and warriors. They were also farmers, merchants, and explorers, who opened up new trade routes across the known world – and beyond, sailing farther afield than any European people before the Portuguese and Spanish explorers of the later 15th century. Nor did they bring only war and looting. Their legal code, social institutions, vibrant new art forms and literature, and skills of ship-building and navigation had great influence on other nations. Vikings are credited with the creation of the European parliamentary model, the English jury system, and even the novel. Swedish Vikings traveled east into Russia, which they called Gardariki, 'kingdom of towns,' and reached Constantinople, where many Viking mercenaries enlisted in the Varangian Guard, the 'Foreign Legion' of the Byzantine Empire. The Danes headed for northern Europe and England, first as pirates, then as settlers. The Norwegians set out to colonize outlying lands, from the Atlantic islands and northern Britain to Iceland, where they founded a new nation which claims today to be Europe's oldest democracy. In c.980 a Viking called Erik the Red (exiled from Norway and then from Iceland 'because of some killings') established a settlement in Greenland – from which, in c.1000, his son Leif the Lucky and others voyaged to 'Vinland' – North America.

Found near Oslo, the 'Gokstad ship' is an ocean-going longship (a replica has crossed the Atlantic) built in c.850. It is 79ft (24m) long and was built to carry 32 rowers.

An iron helmet of Swedish make (compare *pages 30 -31*), dating from 7th-9th centuries.

The figureheads of the Vikings' 'dragon ships' may have struck terror into the victims of their raids – but they are also objects of great artistic merit.

The eyeguards (ornamented with stylized beasts) and crest of the helmet are of bronze. A chainmail mask may have protected the lower face.

A turf walled house like those of Viking Iceland: reconstructed at L'Anse-aux-Meadows, Newfoundland, site of the only definitely known Viking settlement in North America.

❏ From the 10th century, Viking raiders ran a profitable protection racket in England, demanding large bribes (*danegeld*) to stop their raids. Their demands were frequent: a Swedish runestone (like that above) commemorating an 11th century Viking, Ulfr, records his share in three payments of *danegeld*.

❏ Icelandic settlers, perhaps passing their long, dark winters by story telling, were the Vikings' historians, producing records like the *Landnamabok* ('Book of Settlements') on Iceland's colonization; histories (sagas) of their Norwegian ancestors; and, from the 12th century, epic stories of their own people. Once seen as simply historical records, these are now hailed by some as the first novels.

❏ For all their ferocity, the Vikings may be seen as one of the first truly democratic peoples. Their elected chiefs could not go against a majority decision. A 10th century Frank who demanded to speak to the leader of a Viking fleet was told: 'There is no leader: we are all equals.'

Island of a hundred kings

When the Romans withdrew from Britain, Celtic sea raiders from Ireland (which escaped Roman occupation) came seeking plunder. Among their leaders was Niall Ui Niall (d.405), whose clan, the O'Neills, soon became very powerful. But although O'Neill chiefs sometimes claimed to rule the entire country, early medieval Ireland had as many as 100 kings at one time. Petty kings over no more than a few farms gave allegiance to more powerful rulers, who in turn submitted to 'overkings.' By c.800, four provinces under 'high kings' had emerged: Leinster, Munster, Connaught, and Ulster. From 795, Viking seafarers at first raided Ireland, then established permanent settlements, notably Dublin in 841. Some 'overkings' allied with them, but pagan, Norse power in Ireland was broken by the first true 'high king,' Brian Boru (c.940-1014). This Munster prince dominated most of Ireland by c.1002, and in 1014 his army beat the Danes of Dublin under Sitric 'Silky Beard' at Clontarf, where Brian himself fell. An invasion by Magnus III of Norway in 1103 was defeated, but clan warfare after Brian's death had paved the way for conquest by a stronger foe. In 1167 a deposed king of Leinster asked aid from King Henry II of England (who himself claimed to have been granted overlordship of Ireland by the Pope). In 1170 Dublin fell to an English army under Earl Richard de Clare ('Strongbow'); next year, Henry landed and forced the submission of many chiefs. But overall English rule was not achieved until the 17th century: at the end of the medieval period it was largely limited to a zone ('the Pale') around Dublin, where the Irish language, laws, and customs were forcibly suppressed.

The 'Gallarus oratory' in County Kerry is sometimes said to be the oldest surviving Christian church in Ireland, dating from the 8th century; but some authorities say it may have been built as late as the 12th century.

Strange beasts and a grotesque (to modern eyes) human figure ornament the bronze head of a crosier (staff of office) made for an Irish bishop or abbot around the 7th-8th centuries. Irish metalworkers of the period were much influenced by the craftsmen of Anglo-Saxon Britain.

The crosier's history reflects that of Ireland in its time. It was found at Helgö, Sweden, and may have been part of the loot of Viking seafarers, who raided Ireland before they settled there.

The famous 'Tara brooch' was in fact found elsewhere: its name was given by the modern jeweler who first marketed copies. Dating from around 700, it is of bronze overlaid with delicate gold filigree work, ornamented with glass and amber.

From around the 7th century the Rock of Cashel in County Tipperary was the stronghold of the kings of Munster (southwest Ireland). The ruins now seen are of a later time.

❑ Many ancient Irish laws survived the coming of Christianity in the 5th century, including freedom to divorce by common consent. This gave ambitious women the chance to make a career of marriage. One such was Queen Gormlaith, who wedded three kings in succession – Olaf Curan, Viking king of Dublin; Malachy, king of Meath; and Brian Boru – and almost made a fourth royal alliance with Earl Sigurd, ruler of Orkney.

❑ It was a custom to distinguish between Irish rulers of the same name by semi-official nicknames. The very many O'Neill rulers had such names as Aedh 'White Hair,' Aedh 'the Agued [Feverish],' Domnal 'the Young Ox,' and Murketagh 'of the Leather Cloaks' (from his soldiers' dress). The Aedh O'Neill who ruled in Ulster in 1176-77 cannot have been pleased with his nickname: *Macaemh Tóinlensg* ('the Lazy Assed').

❑ Ireland acquired what is now one of its most famous landmarks in 1446, when Lord Cormac McCarthy of Muskerry completed his castle at Blarney, near Cork. Set in its walls is a limestone rock which is said to confer the gift of persuasive speech ('blarney') on all who kiss it. The legend of the 'Blarney Stone' may date from c.1600, when another Cormac McCarthy made many convincing excuses to delay surrendering the castle to an English force.

43

The wandering Jews

Pointed or horned caps, like those seen here, were among the distinguishing marks that medieval Jews had to wear in most countries.

Dispersed throughout the world, the Jews were still united by their faith. Here, as shown by the 15th century Flemish painter Dirck Bouts, a few gather to celebrate Passover.

'Jews shall enjoy no honors. Their status shall reflect the baseness they have elected and desired.' This cruel law of the Byzantine Emperor Justinian was taken up by many medieval rulers. The diaspora ('dispersion') of the Jewish people after the destruction of Judaea by the Romans in the 1st-2nd centuries made them wanderers throughout the world – and persecution soon began. European rulers found the Jews a useful scapegoat. Claiming that those who had 'killed Christ' were capable of any crime, they blamed Jews for all kinds of political, economic, and social problems. Jews could live only in certain areas (ghettos); must wear distinguishing marks (yellow patches; a yellow, pointed or horned cap); and were restricted to certain trades, notably usury (money-lending at interest; forbidden to Christians by the church). Debt-ridden rulers encouraged immigration by Jewish merchants and bankers, from whom they extorted money in return for 'protection.' Often this failed: England saw nationwide killings of Jews in 1189, when at York c.150 Jews committed suicide to escape a lynch mob. Crusaders slaughtered Jews throughout Europe and the Middle East; there were more massacres when Jews were blamed for the plague called the Black Death. By the 14th century, most Ashkenazim (Yiddish-speaking European Jews) had resettled in eastern Europe. Muslim countries, notably Moorish Spain, showed more tolerance. But by the late 15th century all Spain was Christian, and many Sephardim (Jews speaking Ladino, a Spanish tongue) had to seek sanctuary in the Muslim lands of North Africa and the Middle East.

Clifford's Tower at York in northern England is a grim reminder of medieval racism. In 1189 c.150 Jews falsely accused of ritual murder took refuge there – then killed themselves to escape a Christian lynch mob.

In the late Middle Ages El Transito synagogue, Toledo, Spain, was forced to become a Christian church. Today it is once again a Jewish place of worship.

Dwellers in the ghetto (Jewish quarter) of Venice worshiped in this synagogue in the late medieval period.

❏ The Falasha ('black Jews') of Ethiopia are sometimes said to be a 'lost tribe of Israel.' They are more likely descended from native Ethiopians converted to Judaism around the 6th century. Judaism traditionally does not seek converts – but Jewish missionaries appear to have worked in northern Africa at this time, even converting Dhu Nuwas, pre-Islamic Arab king of Yemen.

❏ A common slander against Jews was that they kidnaped Christian children for use in ritual sacrifice. Not until the 20th century did the Catholic Church condemn the cults of child 'saints' – like Little Hugh of Lincoln (d.1255) and Simon of Trento (d.1475) – supposedly murdered by Jews whose rites called for the use of Christian blood.

❏ At Béziers, France, Easter Week was marked by a kind of medieval 'trick or treat:' townsmen had the right to stone Jews' houses unless the occupants paid ransom. Jews in Toulouse had to elect one of their number to take a ritual beating in the cathedral on Good Friday. France expelled all Jews in 1392; England had done so in 1290.

❏ A medieval Jewish joke tells of a rabbi who visited Rome – and became a Christian. He said that a faith that could survive the evil he had seen in the Pope's city must indeed be the true one.

The heirs of St. Peter

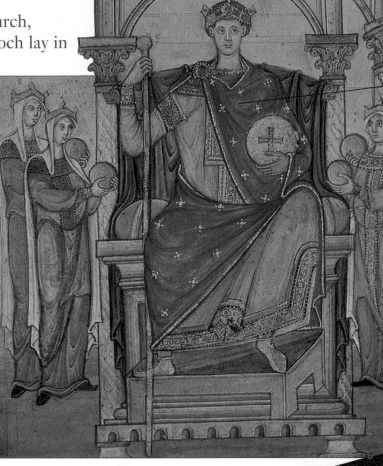

Of the five great centers of the early Christian Church, Constantinople, Jerusalem, Alexandria, and Antioch lay in the East. The one Western center, Rome, claimed supremacy. Christ had said of St. Peter: 'Upon this rock I build my church.' Peter's heirs as bishops of Rome claimed sole right to the title 'pope' (*papa*, 'father'), used by all bishops until c.500, and supreme religious authority. Acceptance of the claim to supremacy owed much to Pope Gregory I 'the Great' (in office 590-604). In England, whose conversion Gregory began, and much of Europe, the fact that most missionaries were sent by Rome served to establish the Roman popes' primacy. Rome began to seek political power also. In 962 Pope John XII crowned Otto I of Germany as Holy Roman Emperor. Rome intended the Empire to be an alliance in which the Emperor would use worldly power to assert the Church's spiritual authority. Instead it led to long conflict between the rival factions of the Pope (Guelphs) and the Emperor (Ghibellines). After the schism (split) of 1054, when Eastern Catholics broke from the West to form the Orthodox Church, the papacy's spiritual power reached its height. Gregory VII (called Hildebrand; in office 1073-85) forced Emperor Henry IV to do penance before him; Innocent III's Lateran Council of 1215 firmly established Rome's religious supremacy. But political claims made by Boniface VIII in 1300 led to the papacy's exile ('hijacked' by France) to Avignon in 1309-78, and to a schism (1379-1417) that saw election of rival popes in Avignon and Rome. Some truly holy men wore the 'Fisherman's Ring,' but many medieval popes were power hungry politicians rather than priests.

The Holy Roman Empire in c.1150

The Holy Roman Empire, smaller and less cohesive successor to Charlemagne's Frankish Empire (compare map on *page 28*), is shown here at about its greatest extent. Throughout its history it was ruled by German or Austrian emperors.

St. John Lateran, founded by Pope Melchiades in the 4th century (the present building is of a much later date), was the papacy's major basilica (cathedral) until 1307.

A 10th century manuscript, product of the Western cultural revival of his time, shows Otto I the Great of Germany (912-73) after his crowning as Holy Roman Emperor in 962.

Rome's Castel Sant'Angelo, begun in A.D. 139 as the mausoleum of Emperor Hadrian, later became a papal fortress and prison.

Angels made by the great sculptor Gian Bernini (1598-1680) line the bridge leading to the fortress.

❏ Although all monks and priests took vows of celibacy (sexual abstinence), the Church did not strictly enforce this until after 1100. (The last pope known to have been married was Adrian II, elected in 867). The rule was often broken: a number of popes appointed their 'nephews' (illegitimate sons) to high office – from which we derive the word 'nepotism,' unfair favoritism towards kinfolk.

❏ Papal corruption flourished in the 10th century, when six popes were assassinated and two died in prison. Marozia (d.938), mistress of Pope Sergius III, had Pope John X (her mother's lover) deposed and her own illegitimate son elected as John XI. Her 18-year-old grandson became Pope John XII in 955. In 963 he was deposed by Emperor Otto I. John XII had, among other crimes, run a brothel in the papal palace, publicly drunk the health of the devil, and castrated a cardinal.

❏ Only one Englishman has ever been pope. Nicholas Breakspear (1100-59), son of a priest (before the celibacy rule), rose through monastic ranks to achieve the office as Adrian IV in 1154.

❏ Ruled from 1274 onwards by the predominantly Austrian Habsburg line, the Holy Roman Empire endured (in name rather than power from about the 17th century) until the early 19th century.

'El Cid,' champion of Spain

Inspired by their new Muslim faith, North African Arabs (whom southern Europeans called Moors) invaded southern Spain. By the 8th century most of modern Spain and Portugal made up the state of al-Andalus, ruled by the Arab Ummayad emirs. Their capital at Cordoba, a magnificent center of Islamic culture, was reckoned in c.1000 to be Western Europe's largest, richest city. After the fall of the Umayyads in 1031 the Moorish empire split into rival kingdoms. Now began the *Reconquista* ('reconquest'): an onslaught on Moorish Spain by the Christian kingdoms to the north. Although the reconquest was not completed until the 15th century, its earlier years produced Spain's national hero, Rodrigo Díaz de Vivar (c.1043-99), called 'El Cid [Campeador]' ('My Lord [the Warrior]'). The epic *Poema de Mio Cid* (composed c.1140-60) portrays him as a 'perfect knight': brave, honorable, loyal, gentle. The truth may be different. He was an army commander under King Alfonso VI of Castile, but in 1081 was outlawed on suspicion of treason. He became a mercenary whose band of heavy cavalry hired out to fight for Christian or Muslim rulers alike. His greatest feat, the capture of Valencia from the Moors in 1094, was accomplished with the aid of a largely Muslim army; he had the city's governor burned alive and massacred many citizens; and although governing in Alfonso's name, he made Valencia his own private kingdom. Legend says that even in death El Cid was victorious: his body, armed and armored, strapped upright on his white horse, terrified a Moorish army into retreat. In fact, Valencia was retaken by the Moors soon after his death.

The Moorish stronghold of Murviedro (modern Sagunto) in Valencia fell to El Cid in 1098 after a long siege, ending Muslim hopes of retaking the province.

These magnificent columns and arches formed part of La Mezquita, the Great Mosque of Cordoba, begun in the 8th century. After 1236, in the 'reconquest' of Moorish Spain, it became a cathedral.

On the fortress hill at Sagunto a medieval castle incorporates remains of Roman and Moorish defenses.

The map shows Moorish Spain (al-Andalus) at about its greatest extent under the Ummayads, when Arab armies often raided at will into Christian areas. The Christian 'reconquest' took more than 400 years, until the fall of Granada in 1492.

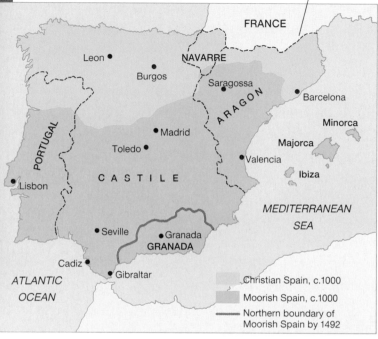

❑ Like most semi-legendary heroes, El Cid (above) had a famous horse – with an unlikely name: Babieca ('Stupid'). It was a gift from his godfather, who is said to have uttered this exclamation when the young hero chose what was apparently the ugliest, clumsiest colt from the string of horses offered to him.

❑ However bloody handed El Cid may have been, he was matched by the Moorish chief Yusuf ibn-Tashfin, whose Almoravid (North African Berber) horde invaded Spain in 1086. His 'Black Guards' (light cavalry, wearing black robes) routed King Alfonso VI's army at Zalaca. Ibn-Tashfin had all the dead decapitated, and with the heads built mounds from the summit of which *muezzins* (Muslim holy men) gave the call for prayers to thank Allah.

❑ El Cid is said to have founded Spain's first leprosy hospital in 1067, after taking pity on a beggar who revealed himself as the Biblical leper Lazarus and promised the hero God's favor.

Christian knights repulse a charge by Moors: an episode of the 'reconquest' from a 13th century manuscript.

Turbans and dark skins here characterize the Muslim warriors who battled to hold southern Spain.

Year of the warlords: 1066

The Bayeux Tapestry shows Norman craftsmen at work on a 'longship' for the invasion of England.

Cnut the Great's empire of Denmark, Norway, and England broke up on his death in 1035. In England, Saxon rule was restored from 1042 under King Edward 'the Confessor' (so called for his piety; he spent much time confessing his sins to priests). In January 1066, when Edward died childless, England was claimed by Harald Hardrada of Norway (as a successor to Cnut), and Duke William 'the Bastard' of Normandy, to whom Edward may have promised the crown. Their claims were jumped by Earl Harold Godwinson, Edward's brother-in-law and England's most powerful noble, who had himself crowned as Harold II. He expected a Norman invasion on the south coast, but Hardrada attacked first, landing in northeast England. Harold marched north with his *huscarles* (household troops) and *fyrd* (militia) and defeated Hardrada at Stamford Bridge, near York, on September 25. Three days later William landed in the south. Harold made another forced march, and on October 14 the armies met near Hastings. William had c.3,000 horsemen and c.6,000 archers and spearmen; Harold's men, all on foot, numbered c.10,000, but most were untrained *fyrd* men. Harold took the high ground, forming a shield ring against which William hurled his heavy horse in vain – until the ring weakened when some Saxons broke away to loot valuable chain mail from the Norman dead. Norman archers poured in arrows; then Norman horsemen broke the defensive wall. Many *fyrd* men slipped away, but the *huscarles* swung their 5ft (1.5m) battleaxes in defense of their banners, 'Dragon of Wessex' and 'Fighting Man,' even after Harold fell. On Christmas Day, 1066, King William I 'the Conqueror' of England was crowned in London's Westminster Abbey.

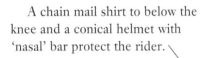

A chain mail shirt to below the knee and a conical helmet with 'nasal' bar protect the rider.

The long handled battleax and stout spear were the weapons favored by Harold's men, who fought on foot against Norman cavalry.

As the Bayeux Tapestry shows, both Normans and Saxons made use of long, kite shaped shields made of wood and leather.

Battle Abbey, near Hastings, was founded by William to commemorate his victory over King Harold on nearby Senlac (Sandlake) Hill.

The great keep of the Tower of London was built for King William from c.1076. Since Henry III (1207-72) had it whitewashed, it has been known as the 'White Tower.'

A Latin caption identifies the horseman with a mace as Odo, Duke William's half-brother.

FACT FILE

❑ King Harald III Hardrada ('Stern Counsel;' literally 'Tough') well merited his name. He had commanded the Varangian Guard (Emperor's bodyguard) at Constantinople and won victories in North Africa and Russia. He is said to have stood some 7ft (2.13m) tall: at Stamford Bridge, Harold promised him 'six feet of English ground, or as much more as he is taller than other men.' Hardrada died in the battle, and of 300 ships that brought his men to England under the banner 'Land Waster' (Odin's black raven), only 24 were needed to carry home survivors.

❑ The Bayeux Tapestry (not a true tapestry, but an embroidered linen strip 231ft (70m) long and 19.5in (49.5cm) deep) was worked soon after William's victory. One section shows a warrior (traditionally Harold) struck in the eye by an arrow, while a second Saxon is cut down by a mounted Norman. Most scholars now believe the second man represents Harold.

❑ William ordered a thorough inventory of his new kingdom. The Saxons, believing they would be heavily taxed on all their possessions, fiercely resisted, and were as fiercely punished. It is generally believed that their comparison between this severity and the biblical Last Judgement caused William's census of 1086 to become known as the 'Domesday [Doomsday] Book.'

Castles rise and fall

Although the huge earthworks thrown up by earlier peoples are sometimes called 'castles,' true castles originated in France in the 9th century. The earliest were 'motte and bailey' type. The motte was a cone of earth, typically c.45ft (14m) high and with a flat top c.60ft (18m) in diameter, on which stood a wooden tower. Excavation for the motte made a deep ditch (filled with water if available) that encircled the bailey, a palisaded enclosure in which stood stock pens and storehouses. The tower could only be reached from the bailey via a bridge over the ditch and a steep, easily defensible path. From the 12th century earth and timber fortifications were replaced by stone. A wet or dry ditch (moat) surrounded a curtain wall pierced by a single fortified gate, often with drawbridge and portcullis (a grating lowered to block the entrance). Inside the wall, the bailey was dominated by a massive tower, the donjon (or keep). From the 13th century, when Crusaders brought back word of the sophisticated fortifications and siege engines of the East, the castle reached its strongest form. In 'concentric castles,' the donjon stood within two or more rings of defensive walls incorporating round towers (more resistant to battering rams, catapults, and cannon than square ones) and machicolations (projecting platforms for archers and missile throwers). The development of heavy cannon was not the main reason for the castles' decline. Castles were a product of feudal times, when kings relied on nobles to maintain local law and order, and nobles needed refuges from their enemies. As the power of centralized government increased, castles lost their importance.

A castle for the age of cannon: this coastal fortification at Deal, Kent, was built for King Henry VIII in c.1540.

From two levels, each of six semi-circular bastions round a central keep, cannon command a wide, dry moat.

Its outer walls rising from a deep moat (it was originally built on a lake island), Caerphilly Castle, Wales, raised in the late 13th century, was among Britain's strongest.

Concentric defense at its strongest: an inner ring of curtain walls and towers surrounds the central keep.

As now seen, Dover Castle, with its massive barbican (gatehouse), dates from c.1260 – but the Romans fortified this site before c.300.

An early concentric castle, Dover stands on a motte (mound) like those of earlier, simpler fortresses.

FACT FILE

❏ The great defensive strength of castles obscures the fact that their true function was an offensive one. The most important role of the castle was as a cavalry base, from which mounted men could ride out to control the surrounding countryside.

❏ It is a mistake to think that all the ruined castles now seen in Europe (above) fell to dramatic sieges. So long as they were well provisioned, most castles could withstand a siege indefinitely, even if cannon were used. Most castles that were captured fell by treachery, or from shortage of food or water, rather than by assault. Many are now in ruins because, from the later 15th century, rulers seeking to deny strongholds to potential rebels made it a policy to 'slight' (demilitarize) castles.

❏ By the 13th century, rulers wary of rebellion had introduced a system of 'planning permission.' A noble who wished to strengthen his residence had to apply for a 'licence to crenellate;' i.e., to build battlements with crenellations (notches) that provided shelter in which a crossbowman or, later, a handgunner could reload.

God's glorious houses

One good aspect of the Crusades was the spread of new ideas from East to West. Among these innovations were improved building techniques, with efficient cranes and hoists. These contributed from the 11th century to the building of great cathedrals and abbeys on such a scale that Europe was said to be 'clothed in a white robe of churches.' In 1050-1350, France alone quarried more stone for cathedrals than ancient Egypt had for pyramids. Romantic legend says medieval craftsmen worked 'for the love of God.' In fact, skilled stone workers commanded high wages and would down tools if pay or conditions were not to their liking. The Church had to undertake massive fund raising to finance its glorious houses of God, begging donations from rich and poor alike and raising money by the sale of indulgences (pardons for sins). Nôtre-Dame, Paris, was funded 'with the farthings [smallest coins] of old women' – and a donation from the prostitutes' guild. Earlier church design copied the public buildings of classical Rome. 'Romanesque' churches had thick walls, fat columns, and heavy, rounded arches. After 1140, with the Abbey of St. Denis, France, the 'Gothic' style appeared. Masons learned to spread the weight of stone across a framework of stone ribs (cross-vaulting) and delicate pointed arches. This created taller, more graceful churches, with slender pillars, spires, and many stained glass windows. Classical severity gave way to decoration: the 550 statues ('smiling angels') of Rheims Cathedral; the great rose window of Nôtre-Dame; the soaring columns of the rebuilt Westminster Abbey. A large cathedral might contain 10,000 figures, painted on glass and carved in stone.

The rose window (12th -13th centuries) of Chartres Cathedral, France, is a masterpiece of stained glass – a decorative art in which medieval craftsmen have never been excelled.

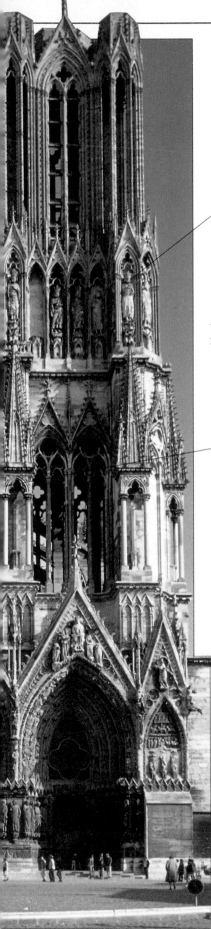

Praising God for centuries, the 'smiling angels' of Rheims, north east France, have graced the city's High Gothic cathedral since its erection in c.1210-70.

At Rheims a great rose window, rather than sculptured decoration, fills the tympanum (the space between the top of the door and the arch above it) on the twin-towered west facade.

After c.1350 English architects created 'Perpendicular' style. Their graceful 'fan vaulting' was first used in the cloisters of Gloucester Cathedral.

Peasants thresh corn: a medieval misericord in an English church. Misericords ('mercy seats') were supports on the undersides of normal seats, on which worshipers could lean when they were supposed to stand. Since they were not normally visible, they were often carved with scenes (sometimes humorous) from everyday life.

❏ Although the Roman Catholic Church now disapproves of the 'secret society' of Freemasonry, 'free masons' may have had their origin in the wealthy and powerful trades guilds (unions) of medieval building workers.

❏ Egypt's Great Pyramid, at c.480ft (146m), was the world's tallest structure for nearly 4,000 years. It was first overtopped by Lincoln Cathedral, England. The spire of Lincoln's central tower, begun in c.1307 and destroyed by a storm in 1548, rose to 525ft (160m).

❏ England's Salisbury Cathedral claims to house the world's oldest working mechanical clock (above), dating from 1386. Found derelict in 1929, it was carefully restored and preserves much of its original mechanism. Like most medieval clocks, it has no dial: the first known 'public dial' clock did not appear (in Oxford, England) until 1505.

Holy wars: the Crusades

Medieval maps often show Jerusalem at the center of the world, for it was the 'Holy City' of Christ, capital of the 'Holy Land' of Palestine. Christians believed that a pilgrimage to the holy places in Palestine would win them forgiveness for all their sins. From c.300 Palestine was part of the Byzantine Empire, but in the 7th century it was captured by the Arabs. Although they were Muslims, they allowed Christians to visit the holy places. But in the 11th century Palestine fell to the Seljuk Turks, warlike Muslims who killed Christian pilgrims. Pope Urban II (1042-99) urged European Christians to free the Holy Land by force. The badge of the Christian armies was the cross (Latin: *crux*), so their campaigns were called 'Crusades.' Eight Crusades were launched between 1096 and 1272. The First Crusade (1096-99) ended in the capture of Jerusalem, and the Crusaders set up their own kingdoms in the Holy Land. But over the years the Crusaders were weakened by quarrels between their leaders. The great Muslim general Saladin (1137-93) recaptured Jerusalem in 1187, and the Third Crusade (1189-91), one of whose leaders was King Richard I ('Lionheart') of England, failed to retake it. Although some Crusaders were truly religious, others were more interested in money. Armies on their way to the Middle East sometimes looted towns in Eastern Europe. During the Fourth Crusade (1202-04), Constantinople itself was sacked. After the death of King Louis IX of France (St. Louis) during the Eighth Crusade (1270-72), Acre, the last Crusader stronghold in the Holy Land, fell to the Muslims in 1291.

Crusaders and Muslims alike often wore helmets of this pattern.

Christian knights – one eagerly gripping a mace in hope of cracking pagan skulls – embark for the Holy Land; a 15th century painting.

The conical helmet (a *spangenhelm* to modern armorers) is made of iron plates on iron ribs. As well as cheek pieces, a chain mail aventail ('veil') may have hung from it to guard neck and shoulders.

Based on a Roman model, the *spangenhelm* was favored especially by the Seljuks ('Saracens'), light cavalry who otherwise usually wore little armor.

Stores are loaded aboard the galley. The first two Crusades (1096-99; 1147-49) traveled overland, devastating parts of eastern Europe with their foraging for supplies.

The artist shows knights so zealous that they are prepared to row themselves. Perhaps some did – but the mariners of Venice and Genoa made huge profits carrying Crusaders.

A 14th century depiction of Saladin, Kurdish ruler of Egypt and Syria in 1175-93, whose skill, courage, and courtesy became legendary.

A cross on the jupon (short jacket worn over armor) is the Crusader's emblem.

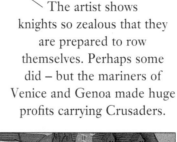

A medieval artist's realistic view of the Crusaders' capture of Jerusalem in 1099, when Muslim and Jewish citizens were massacred.

❑ The Sixth Crusade (1228-29) was led by Holy Roman Emperor Frederick II (1194-1250) (above) , called *Stupor Mundi* ('Wonder of the World') for his wide ranging abilities. His force included 50 'landing craft' with hinged ramps (his own design), but he avoided violence and gained Jerusalem by treaty with the Saracens. For this peaceful achievement, militant Christians denounced him as 'Antichrist' and Popes Gregory IX and Innocent IV called for 'crusades' to be made against him.

❑ In the tragic 'Children's Crusade' of 1212, c.50,000 French and German peasants, many of them children, were inspired by fanatical preachers to set out for Palestine. Many died of hunger and disease; others were kidnaped by shipowners who promised them free transport, then sold them into slavery in Egypt and North Africa.

Merchant adventurers

One of the mightiest medieval states was founded by refugees from barbarian invaders in Italy in the 6th century. They fled to small islands in a lagoon on the Adriatic coast, and in this sheltered refuge built up the Republic of Venice, by the 10th century a sea power rich on trade between the Byzantine Empire and the West. Its war galleys swept the Adriatic and eastern Mediterranean of pirates, opening sea lanes for ships carrying Oriental silks and spices. In the Crusades, Venice profited by carrying soldiers and supplies to the Holy Land – and by political scheming. Venice engineered the Crusaders' capture of Constantinople in 1204; then grabbed one-third of the stricken Byzantine Empire. In 1380 its fleet destroyed that of its one great rival, Genoa. Officially ruled by an elected Doge (Duke) through a senate, the republic was from c.1310 controlled by a 'secret society:' the Council of Ten, made up of its richest merchants. But it had wealth enough to keep its citizens contented and, unlike other Italian city-states, preserved its independence until French conquest in 1797. Venetian ships at Bruges (now in Belgium) – Europe's major trading port until its harbor silted up in the 15th century – met the sturdy cogs (armed merchantmen) of the Hanseatic League (Hansa). This federation of North German ports, founded by Lübeck and Hamburg in 1241, dominated the Baltic and North Sea trade. At its height in the 14th century the Hansa embraced some 100 towns. Its goods were exempt from customs; its offices abroad, like its London 'Steelyard' (*Staalhaf,* 'sample warehouse'), were independent 'colonies;' its depots extended from London to Novgorod in Russia. The growth of Dutch sea power sent the League into decline from the 16th century.

Modern Venice preserves much of its medieval splendor. The 300ft (91m) high Campanile (bell tower), dating from the 9th century (but much restored), rises over St. Mark's Square.

The bustling waterfront of Venice in an illustration of 1338. Galleys and sailing ships crowd the roadstead; ashore, the lion of St. Mark, emblem of the city's patron, is seen on its pillar.

A modern reconstruction of a small but sturdy Hansa cog.

The magnificent Palazzo Ducale (Doge's Palace), built in the 14th century, was the seat of the republic's government.

Broad beamed and high sided, the cog could be quickly and easily converted into a warship by adding 'castles' at bow and stern.

From the 7th century until 1797, the Doge (duke) ruled Venice.

❏ Symbol of Venice's maritime might was the *Bucentaur* ('Golden Barque'), the huge state galley. Every year, from around the 12th century until 1797, the Doge flung a gold ring into the sea from the galley, saying: 'We wed thee, sea, in token of perpetual domination.'

❏ In 1202 Venice agreed to carry men of the Fourth Crusade to the Holy Land, but the Crusaders could not pay their fare. The Venetians made a deal: a Crusader army in Venetian ships descended on Zara (Zadar), an Adriatic port that was cutting into Venetian profits, and sacked it. The Pope protested vainly at the destruction of a peaceful, Christian city. The next year, 93-year-old Doge Enrico Dandolo personally led the first Crusader-Venetian assault on Constantinople.

❏ Hanseatic seamen earned trading privileges by keeping the northern sea lanes free from pirates. In 1422 Hansa ships fought a three day battle off Heligoland with a pirate fleet under an outlaw knight called Stertebeken ('Big Mug,' from his capacity for ale). Stertebeken was captured and beheaded in Hamburg.

❏ One ruler who tried to limit Hansa powers, Waldemar IV of Denmark, gave in after a naval struggle (1361-70) which ended with a Hansa fleet threatening an invasion of his capital city, the port of Copenhagen.

Charter of liberty

Richard I's extravagant Crusades left his brother and heir to the throne of England, King John (1167-1216), short of money in 1199. John's vile temper and his rumored murder of a rival for the throne, his young nephew Arthur of Brittany, made him personally unpopular. He alienated his barons (noblemen) by heavy taxation for unsuccessful campaigns in France; his attempt to limit the Church's power put England under papal interdict (denial of all religious rites) for six years. When he tried to tax the barons still more, threat of rebellion forced him to accept a program limiting royal power. At Runnymede near London, on June 15, 1215, John agreed to *Magna Carta* ('Great Charter'). Intended by the barons to protect their own interests – most cared little for the rights of commoners – *Magna Carta* has become a symbol of human rights, influencing government systems that include the U.S. Constitution. Clauses 39-40 said justice must not be denied, sold, or delayed: no one should be imprisoned without cause; all should have a prompt, fair trial. When John tried to annul the Charter, some barons invited Prince Louis of France to take the throne, but major civil war was averted by John's death and Louis's defeat by supporters of John's son, 9-year-old King Henry III (1207-72). But Henry's later refusal to accept more reforms led to the Barons' War of 1264-67. Henry was at first defeated, and in 1264-65 England was ruled by Simon de Montfort (1208-65), Earl of Leicester. Seeking popular suppport, de Montfort called important commoners to sit in Parliament (a term then new) for the first time. Although he was soon defeated and killed by royal forces, he is now honored in Britain as 'Father of the House of Commons.'

King John (r.1199-1216) was an unlucky monarch. Fighting French invasion, he lost the English crown jewels, sunk in quicksand that swallowed his baggage train.

John's effigy on his tomb in Worcester Cathedral is far lovelier than his reputation in life, when he was called tyrant and murderer.

John pursues a stag in a royal forest; a 14th century illustration. Huge tracts of England were then preserved as hunting grounds for the nobility.

Simon de Montfort is shown as a huntsman on his official seal. Although married to King Henry III's sister, he led many of England's nobles against the king.

In medieval times most important documents were sealed, not signed.

Although it was not primarily intended to benefit the common people, England's *Magna Carta* of 1215 is often said to be the most important statement ever made in the cause of civil rights.

❏ As the youngest son of King Henry II, John was given no territories by his father and was nicknamed 'Lackland.' As king, he lost Normandy and Anjou to France in 1204 and got an even more insulting name: 'Softsword.' In fact, John was a brave but rash soldier, and, when he took the trouble, a good administrator: he was the first English monarch to order written records of government decisions to be kept. Like Richard III, he got much of his bad reputation from Shakespeare's portrayal – and from the fact that he features as a villain (quite wrongly) in 'Robin Hood' tales.

❏ John was a compulsive traveler: he owned some 80 castles and hunting lodges and spent much of his time shuttling between them (partly to make himself a more difficult target for his enemies). Forced to make economies, he decreed that the many prostitutes who accompanied his court must do the laundry in addition to their normal duties. He did everything in a hurry: his death is said to have been caused by a surfeit (a huge meal, eaten very quickly) of peaches and cider.

❏ John agreed to *Magna Carta* by affixing his seal. He may not have been able to write his name. Many medieval monarchs and noblemen considered that reading and writing were 'wimpish' skills fit only for clerks.

The merciless Mongols

In the 13th century an 'unknown' people conquered the largest empire the world has known, from the Danube basin in Hungary to the Pacific. Before c.1200 the Mongols, whom Europeans called Tatars (Tartars), were wandering herdsmen in Manchuria, Mongolia, and Siberia, fighting tribal wars over pasturage. They were forcibly united by a political and military genius, Temujin (c.1167-1227), called Genghis Khan ('Mighty Ruler'). He built up a rigidly disciplined army of perhaps 150,000 horsemen, armed with bow, lance, and sword, and uniformed in black leather. In 1211, his way prepared by a huge, efficient spy system, Genghis attacked the Ch'in Empire in China. By 1227, when he took Peking, his conquest may have cost the lives of 90 per cent (perhaps c.30,000,000) of north China's people. Persia (Iran) and most of Russia also fell. Merciless in war, Genghis was a strict but fairly liberal ruler. He enforced laws aimed at encouraging trade and industry and, pagan himself, tolerated all religions. His policies were continued by his grandson Kublai Khan (1215-94), who founded the Mongol Yüan Dynasty in China in 1279. Mongol conquests raised the 'Islamic curtain' that hampered contact between East and West: in 1260 the European traveler Marco Polo was able safely to make a 140 day journey from the Black Sea to Kublai's court at Peking. Later Mongol rulers lacked the ability of Genghis and Kublai. The Yüan Dynasty was overthrown in 1368 in favor of the native Chinese Ming Dynasty (1368-1644), and after c.1300 the rest of the Mongol Empire broke up, largely because its western khans became Muslims and would not obey a pagan Great Khan. But Mongol dynasties remained in power in some parts of the East – notably India – until after 1500.

Ruthless in pursuit of power, Genghis Khan was one of the most successful war leaders – and one of the most able rulers – of all time.

A vassal kneels to pay tribute to the master of the world, shown here in a 15th century Persian miniature.

From the Mongol heartland around Karakorum, fierce horsemen subdued this mighty empire – briefly made even larger, although less cohesive, under Genghis Khan's successors. Expansion into Europe was checked in 1260 by defeat by the Mamelukes (Egyptian Muslims) near Damascus.

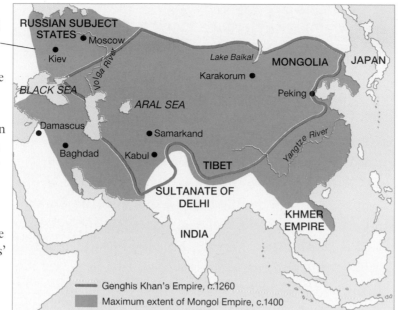

Genghis Khan's Empire, c.1260
Maximum extent of Mongol Empire, c.1400

The deeply curved composite bow was the Mongol warriors' main strike weapon. In battle, they aimed first at horses rather than men, thus destroying the enemy's power of maneuver.

A warrior with a mace wears a raw silk tunic: the material was found to lessen the 'hold' of arrows.

Armor of boiled leather protects a spearman, who will mop up enemy troops unseated by the Mongol archers.

FACT FILE

❑ Genghis Khan is said to have defined the joys that make life worth living as follows: 'To cut my enemies to pieces, drive them before me, seize their possessions, see the tears of those who love them, and **** their wives and daughters.'

❑ Hulagu (1217-65), grandson of Genghis, completed the conquest of Persia (Iran). Islam praised his extermination of the 'Assassins,' drug-fueled Muslim heretics who had terrorized the region for more than a century. But Hulagu hated Muslims, and in 1258 took the great Muslim city of Baghdad. In a 17 day orgy, most of its c.100,000 people were murdered. Its ruler, Caliph al Mustasim, was wrapped in a carpet – to avoid spilling royal blood – and trampled to death by Mongol horsemen (below).

❑ Another of Genghis's grandsons, Batu (d.1256), ruled western and southern Russia from a great tented camp on the Volga River. Batu's tent was golden, and his state became known as the 'Golden Horde.' The name is sometimes wrongly applied to the huge Mongol armies.

The birth of 'Holy Russia'

The 'Holy Face,' a magnificent 14th century icon (devotional painting) in Moscow's Uspensky Cathedral. Christianity came to Russia by way of Byzantium in the 9th-10th centuries.

The great medieval trade route between Northern Europe and Constantinople ran via lakes and rivers lying between the Gulf of Finland and the Black Sea. Around 862 a Varangian (Viking) adventurer called Rurik set up a 'princedom' along these waterways. His people were called 'Rus,' and their territory, centering on the fortified settlements of Novgorod, Smolensk, and Kiev, became known as Russia. Unlike some medieval tales, this traditional account of the birth of a great nation is probably close to the truth. The first important Russian state, Kiev on the Dnieper River, was founded in c.882. Its great period as a center of trade and culture dates from 988, when Prince Vladimir I (955-1015) forcibly converted Kiev to Orthodox Christianity to cement an alliance with Constantinople. Thus was born 'Holy Russia,' to grow to a sprawling empire whose survival for centuries owed much to the unity imposed by its Orthodox faith. Kiev fell to the Mongols (Tatars) in 1240, but it had already been eclipsed by Novgorod and Vladimir-Suzdal.

Novgorod's great Prince Alexander Nevsky (c.1220-63), whose title came from his victory over Swedish invaders on the Neva River in 1240, also crushed an invasion by the Teutonic Knights (*pages 80-81*) in 1242. Yet he could only preserve his realm by paying homage to Mongol overlords, who in 1252 appointed him 'Grand Prince' of Russia. In the 14th century Novgorod was replaced in importance by Vladimir-Suzdal, whose capital had grown up around a *kremlin* (fortress) founded by Prince Yuri Dolgoruki in 1156. By the end of the Middle Ages, this stronghold, Moscow, was the focus of Russian power.

The splendid crown of Vladimir II Monomach (1053-1125) of Kiev, now preserved in the Kremlin Armory, Moscow, became a symbol of Russian imperial power in the following centuries.

Fur, symbolizing what was then a major source of Kiev's wealth, encircles the crown presented by the Byzantine emperor.

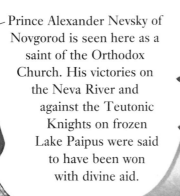

Prince Alexander Nevsky of Novgorod is seen here as a saint of the Orthodox Church. His victories on the Neva River and against the Teutonic Knights on frozen Lake Paipus were said to have been won with divine aid.

Although Alexander Nevsky became (and remains) a Russian national hero, his political power depended on the support of Mongol overlords.

St. Sophia Cathedral, Kiev, was begun in 1037 by Prince Yaroslav. Both its name (from the 'mother church' in Constantinople) and its architecture, with a great central dome surrounded by 12 smaller ones, reflect the influence of Byzantium on early Russia.

❏ Vladimir I of Kiev is venerated as a saint by the Orthodox Church, but his conversion from paganism was for political ends. Legend says he first considered Judaism (but decided he liked pork); then Islam (but that forbids liquor, which he also liked). When he chose Orthodox Christianity he had all pagan idols thrown into the Dnieper River – followed by his subjects, who were herded into the water and forced to undergo mass baptism.

❏ In 1382 a Mongol army burned Moscow to the ground, but it was quickly rebuilt. Its present Kremlin (above) was begun under Grand Prince Ivan III (1462-1505), who imported Italian architects to raise the huge triangular citadel, whose 1.5mi (2.5km) long brick walls are up to 16ft (3.4m) thick. Ivan's grandson, Ivan IV 'the Terrible,' was the first Russian ruler to use the title Tsar (which means 'Caesar,' or 'Emperor'), in 1547.

Scotland's fight for freedom

The Scottish nation took something like its present form under King Malcolm II (reigned 1005-34) and Duncan (r.1034-40). Macbeth (r.1040-57), possibly Duncan's murderer (as Shakespeare tells us), was an able ruler and careful of Scotland's independence. But Malcolm III (r.1057-93) overthrew Macbeth with English aid and married an English princess: English interference grew. To fight it, William I 'the Lion' (r.1165-1214) formed what is still called the 'Auld [Old] Alliance' with France. When infant Queen Margaret, promised as wife to the son of King Edward I of England (r.1272-1307), died in 1290, Edward claimed overlordship of Scotland, invaded, and in 1292 appointed John de Baliol as a puppet ruler. Baliol revolted, so Edward, 'Hammer of the Scots,' annexed Scotland in 1296. The Scots rose under Sir William Wallace (c.1272-1305) and virtually regained independence with a victory at Stirling Bridge in 1297. The next year Wallace was defeated at Falkirk, where English archers broke up Scottish schiltrons (massed blocks of spearmen). He waged a skilfull guerrilla campaign, but in 1305 was betrayed, captured, and executed. His place was taken by ruthless Robert Bruce (1274-1329), who declared himself King Robert I after murdering his main rival, Sir John 'Red' Comyn. After early defeats, Bruce (inspired by watching a spider succeed in spinning a web after many failures, legend says) drove out the English. In 1314 he smashed King Edward II's invading army at Bannockburn, trapping the English in a marsh and trampling them down with his schiltrons. In 1328 King Edward III accepted Scotland's independence, but Scots-English wars continued until the two crowns were united in 1603.

It is interesting to compare this 19th century statue honoring Robert Bruce with the very similar monument to England's King Alfred (*page 33*). Both rulers refused to be discouraged by early defeats.

Bruce won Scotland with his sword, and ruled from 1306 until his death (perhaps from leprosy) in 1329.

The seal of King Robert I (the Bruce) of Scotland, dating from c.1326. Note the heraldic 'Lion of Scotland' on his shield and horse trappings.

The 'Stone of Destiny,' on which Scottish kings were crowned at Scone, near Perth, from c.843 onward, was captured by Edward I of England in 1296 and has ever since (except when briefly 'kidnaped' by Scottish nationalists in 1950-52) rested beneath the English monarchs' Coronation Chair in Westminster Abbey, London.

❏ The English gave Wallace a traitor's death: 'hanged, drawn, and quartered.' He was hanged at the Tower of London, but cut down while still alive to be disemboweled ('drawn') – the sentence said the condemned man's intestines were to be 'torn out and burned before his face' – then beheaded. His body was cut into four 'quarters,' which were displayed in Northumberland and Scotland.

❏ One thing marred Bruce's victory at Bannockburn. At the outset he was charged by a heavily armored knight, Henry de Bohun. He 'cleft de Bohun to the brisket [chin]' – but then sadly told his men: 'Alas! I have broke the haft [handle] of my good ax.'

❏ An old Scots poem describes Bruce's guerrilla tactics, which include denying sleep to the enemy by '*mekill noyis maid on hytht*' ('loud noises from nearby hills'). The bagpipes had probably been introduced into Britain in the 13th century – and some say the poem refers to an early use of Scotland's 'secret weapon!'

❏ Colorful 'Highland dress' now worn at Scots gatherings is largely a romantic invention of the early 19th century, popularized by the novelist Sir Walter Scott. The striped material called tartan dates from as early as c.A.D. 250 – but there is no evidence of specific clan tartans before the 17th century.

Bowmen and gunners

Crossbows – long ranging, hard hitting, but slow firing – are used by Genoese mercenaries on the French side at Crécy, 1346.

English and Welsh archers were famed for their skill with the longbow. The rate of fire of a good longbowman was three or four times that of a crossbowman.

The best medieval missile weapon was also the simplest: the longbow. Ancient bows were short and deeply curved (like those of the medieval East), but in the early 13th century Welsh archers found that greater power came from a bow with a straighter stave of elm or yew wood, some 6ft (1.83m) long. The English adopted the longbow by 1250. It took much strength and years of training to use well, but a good archer could send a 3ft (0.9m) 'clothyard shaft' accurately to a range of 180-240yd (165-220m), shooting six arrows per minute (or up to 12 in a close range 'arrow storm'). The longbow was easy to maintain, unlikely to malfunction, and cheap. The expensive crossbow had slightly more range and penetrative power and demanded less strength and skill, but fired only about two 'quarrels' a minute – the string of the powerful steel 'arbalest' was drawn with handles and pulleys – and was best in defense of fortifications. Gunpowder, known in China by c.800, reached Europe after c.1250. Cannon appeared in the early 1300s: English *crakys* are mentioned in Scotland in 1319. Heavy and slow to move, they might also burst: medieval gunpowder was unreliable, as were early methods of construction. Cannon were mainly used in sieges, but John Zizka of Bohemia (Czechoslovakia) developed a kind of field artillery in c.1410. Leading the Hussites ('heretical' peasants) against large forces of armored horsemen, Zizka mounted cannon on four-wheeled carts, which on the battlefield were linked together to make movable 'wagon forts.' Hand guns, first recorded in the 1330s, came into wider use in the early 1400s, when development of 'matchlocks,' with a slow burning fuze and a trigger mechanism, produced the arquebus, fired from the shoulder.

A German mercenary soldier of the 16th century (dressed for parade rather than battle) carries on his shoulder a matchlock gun: note its trigger mechanism and fuze.

Handgunners in a well equipped French army of the 15th century carry matchlock arquebuses; these had an effective range of about 100yd (90m).

Although fitted with mobile carriages, heavy, cast iron cannon like these were of much more use in siege warfare than on the battlefield.

Pikemen march up to join the army. In battle, one of their tasks was to hold off enemy cavalry attacks while handgunners reloaded.

❑ The longbow called for a pull of c.100lb (45kg), about twice that of a modern sports' bow. Today, archeologists identify the remains of medieval archers from their twisted spines, the result of many years of exerting a massive sidewise pull.

❑ Full plate armor, developed by the 14th century, gave better protection than the earlier chain mail of interlinked metal rings (as many as 30,000 in a knee length mail shirt). Except at fairly short range it was proof against the missiles of most bows or hand guns. But few could afford it: a made to measure suit of best plate armor cost a medieval nobleman about the same as a private jet for his modern equivalent. There was a huge trade in second hand armor.

❑ A suit of finest steel armor (below) weighed less than 60lb (27kg) – but with padded clothing under it was hot and airless. Armored men, especially fighting on foot, sometimes died of heat stroke or suffocation.

The army marches to the stirring strains of fife and drum. Since the earliest times, commanders have recognized the value of martial music in maintaining morale.

The mounted commanders wear plate armor with surfaces curved to deflect missiles. Speed of maneuver kept cavalry effective against the early, slow firing handguns.

Fighting at sea

The galley was the major medieval warship in the Mediterranean, where calm seas and light winds prevailed. The Byzantine 'dromon' ('racer') was propelled by one or two banks of oars, supplemented by a large lateen (triangular) sail on a single mast (two or three masts on later, larger galleys). It carried c.100 rowers and perhaps 150 fighters. In battle, archers and catapults (bow mounted guns from the 15th century) fired as it closed with an enemy at speed, aiming to strike with the ram, a reinforced bow projection underwater. 'Greek fire' was thrown; then the ships grappled for hand to hand combat. Galleys were unsuited to rougher, northern seas, where Viking longships, with 20-30 pairs of oars and a large, square sail, were superb sea going craft, but mainly used as troop transports. Vikings who fought at sea often lashed their ships together to make a platform for a miniature land battle. Their more roomy 'knarr' was a pattern for later 'round ships' like the 'cog.' This had square rigged sails (on two or three masts in later vessels of c.500 tons), and was easily converted from merchant to warship by erecting tall 'castles' at bow and stern. 'Cog' types fought a typical medieval battle at Sluys (Sluis) in 1340. There was little maneuver: some 400 English and French ships, crammed with archers and soldiers, jammed themselves together for close combat. A few guns – small, man-killing 'serpentines' – may have been mounted at Sluys. In 1406 the English *Christopher of the Tower* was one of the first warships purpose built to carry guns, and by c.1450 many had bow or stern mounted 'bombards' (cannon). By c.1500 warships were being built to mount cannon on a lower deck, to fire 'broadside' through gunports in the side.

High 'castles' at bow and stern typify a warship of the later Middle Ages. The stern castle apparently has gunports, but there are none in the hull.

The ship carries a single square rigged sail. It steers by a vertical rudder at the stern – a method introduced from the East after c.1200.

A reconstruction of a Viking *skuta*. This was the smallest type of longship, for fjord and coastal use, crewed by 25-30 men.

The helmsman of a Norman ship guides the vessel with a steering oar on the starboard side, while the crewmen manipulate a lateen (triangular) sail to catch the wind.

The large, square sail is of *wadmal* (homespun flax canvas). Both sail and mast can be lowered and stored.

VIGIO:

Much resembling a Viking longship (the Normans were 'Norsemen'), an invasion craft packed with men and horses heads for the English coast in 1066; from the Bayeux Tapestry.

Shields hang ready to hand at the oar benches. To row was a warrior's honor: a slave who took an oar in emergency was immediately a free man.

FACT FILE

❏ 'Greek fire' is said to have been invented in c.650 (but such compounds were known to the ancients) by a Syrian called Callinias. He sold it to Byzantines – who had him murdered to preserve the secret. A mixture of naphtha, sulfur, and saltpeter, it burnt fiercely, even in contact with water. It was hurled in pots from catapults, or projected from huge bellows and even hand held 'flamethrowers' at closer range.

❏ Until the 12th century Western ships were steered as they had been since ancient times, by one or more broad bladed 'steering oars' projecting from the ship's side (usually on the right, or 'steerboard;' thus 'starboard') near the stern.

❏ All Western ships may have been dwarfed by the Chinese junks of Cheng Ho, who in 1405-29 led seven expeditions (one with 62 ships and 28,000 men) into the Indian Ocean, visiting Ceylon (Sri Lanka), Timor (only c.500mi/805km north of Australia), and southern Africa. Chinese records say his flagship in 1421 was c.540ft (165m) long, with nine masts – the largest sailing vessel of all time.

❏ The word 'Admiral,' for the highest naval rank comes from the Arabic *amir*, 'prince.' From about the 12th century, Muslim naval leaders were given the title *amir-al-bahr*, which means 'prince of the sea.'

The long fight for France

Like the Crusades, which lasted through 195 years, the 'Hundred Years War' between England and France in 1337-1453 was not one war but a serial conflict. It was caused by Edward III (r.1327-77) of England's claim to the French throne; by economic rivalry (both nations wanted control of the rich wool trade); and continuing French support for Scotland. Invading France in 1338, Edward gained control of the sea with naval victory at Sluys. He won land battles at Crécy (1346) and at Poitiers (1356), where the English were led by his son, Edward the 'Black Prince' (1330-76). Both victories were won by English longbowmen, who decisively outshot French crossbowmen, then mowed down massed cavalry attacks. Edward accepted French lands in return for abandoning his claim to the French throne. The Black Prince might have renewed the claim but died before his father. Ten-year-old Richard II succeeded in 1377, and hostilities lapsed. The claim was revived by King Henry V (r.1413-22). Invading France in 1415, he crushed a far larger French army (c.25,000, against c.5,700) at Agincourt, where heavily armored French knights and foot soldiers bogged down and were slaughtered by Henry's c.4,000 archers: some 8,000 French died; only c.500 English. In 1420 Charles VI of France recognized Henry as his heir, but again an early death spoilt England's hopes, when Henry was succeeded by his weak son Henry VI. Inspired by Joan of Arc, a teenaged peasant girl who claimed guidance from Heaven, the French won at Orléans (1429). Even after Joan's capture and death by burning at Rouen in 1431, France gained ground. Bordeaux fell in 1453, leaving England with Calais (held until 1558) as its only French possession.

A 'bombard' (cannon) bound round with metal hoops for strength lies idle as the French advance at Orléans.

Archers (with longbows, although the French normally favored crossbows) aim to pick off the defenders as the attack is launched.

A badge made for his funeral in 1376 shows Edward the 'Black Prince' kneeling before the Holy Trinity. Its border is the 'Garter,' sign of the order of knighthood founded by his father, Edward III.

Scaling ladders are used to storm English defenses at Orléans; May 1429. The victory inspired by Joan of Arc ended a seven month siege and turned the long war in France's favor.

Captured by Burgundians and sold to the English, Joan of Arc was given a 'show trial,' convicted of heresy and witchcraft, and burned. The Roman Catholic Church, whose priests had condemned her, canonized her in 1920.

❑ Edward III's claim to France came from his mother, Isabella (1292-1358), daughter of French King Philip IV and wife of Edward II. This feisty lady — the 'She-wolf of France' — resented her bisexual husband's male favorites (although he gave her four children). She and her lover, Earl Roger Mortimer, rebelled, captured Edward, and had him murdered in 1327. In 1330, 18-year-old Edward III had his mother and her lover arrested. Mortimer was executed; Isabella retired to a country estate with a huge pension.

❑ The 'Black Prince' (above) was not so called until the 16th century, when it was said he had favored black armor. He had not; but a writer of his time had noted that he showed 'black fury' in battle.

Plague and rebellion

Peasants gather in the sheaves; an English stained glass roundel of the 15th century. But all too often the harvests failed.

Famine and plague periodically ravaged the medieval world. Europe was worst hit in 1347-51, when plague carried by infected fleas from black rats that infested trading ships spread from Asia. Bubonic plague (from 'buboes,' swellings, in the armpits and groins of sufferers) darkens the body through hemorrhages beneath the skin, so medieval folk called it the 'Black Death.' Physicians knew no cure and the death toll was immense: perhaps 25,000,000 persons (c.33 per cent of the population) throughout Europe. Britain (perhaps 1,000,000 dead) may have lost one third of its people. Towns were depopulated and trade and industry failed; villages were deserted; crops rotted; livestock too died of plague. Law and morality collapsed: many priests would not help the dying – and the heroic ones who did often died themselves: the Franciscan Order alone lost c.125,000 brothers. After the plague there were severe shortages of goods and labor, so prices and wages soared. Peasants demanded up to eight-fold wage increases and an end to serfdom. When the demands were not fully met, rebellion threatened. In France the peasant *Jacquerie* rose in May-June 1358. A few castles were taken and looted, but the rising was swiftly and bloodily suppressed. In England the Peasants' Revolt of 1381, led by ex-soldier Wat Tyler and rabble rousing priest John Ball, was provoked by tax increases. Tyler's army, c.10,000 strong, marched on London, sacked the City (business quarter), and executed the Archbishop of Canterbury and other officials. King Richard II agreed to meet the rebels, but during the confrontation one of his retinue killed Tyler. The king calmed the peasants with promises – most broken after they were dispersed by force a few days' later.

In winter the hours of labor of the peasant – from sunrise to sunset – were shorter. Here, a sharecropper relaxes with a pipe (tobacco reached Europe in the 16th century), while his wife spins wool.

Only great houses had indoor sanitation in medieval times. Villagers sometimes had a communal earth closet – or simply improvised!

The livestock form part of the family circle: the pig was many peasants' major source of wealth.

Plague victims lie unburied in the streets. The maker of this woodcut for a German *Bible* of 1494 had no hesitation in attributing the pestilence to the wrath of God at the sins of humanity.

Of all medieval monarchs, 'King Death,' with his skull face and an hourglass to show how time runs out, was the one best known to rich and poor alike. He ruled by plague, famine, and war.

The knight's arms will not save him from Death or the wiles of the lurking Devil. Albrecht Dürer's engraving shows how conscious medieval folk were of their frailty and mortality.

❏ Many learned people, including physicians, thought the Black Death had astrological causes, blaming an unfavorable alignment of planets. Others said God was punishing humanity: processions of religious fanatics, 'Flagellants,' wandered Europe, flogging each other as a sign of their repentance. Jews were accused of spreading the plague and even more savagely persecuted.

❏ The *Jacquerie* took their name from '*Jacques Bonhomme*' ('Goodman John'), the nobility's scornful nickname for the long-suffering, uncomplaining peasantry. Although France and England were then at war, English knights helped French nobles put down the rebellion.

❏ The English Peasants' Revolt occurred about the same time that tales of 'Robin Hood' were first set down. The original legends may be based on Robert Hode, an outlaw of York in c.1225; the name, or variations of it, was taken by several later outlaws. The original 'Robin' was neither a nobleman nor a benefactor of the poor; these aspects, like the connection with Kings Richard I and John, Sherwood Forest, and Nottingham, did not appear until the 1500s. There was a 'Friar Tuck' – an outlawed priest called Robert Stafford used the alias – but his deeds were done in Sussex in c.1417-29.

Mountain warriors of Switzerland

Swiss monuments to the national hero William Tell include this old inn sign, showing him with sword in hand and flagon held high.

William Tell is one of the most famous heroes of the Middle Ages. Most people know how, at the order of the tyrannical bailiff Gessler, the crossbow marksman shot an apple from his son's head at 80 paces – then slew Gessler and sparked off the revolt of the Swiss mountain men against Austrian rule. But there is little evidence for Tell's existence: the legend of the 'sure shot' dates back to ancient times and was not applied to Tell until the late 15th century, long after the Swiss revolt. This began in 1291, when Switzerland was part of the Holy Roman Empire ruled by the Austrian Habsburg family. The cantons (states) of Schwyz (which gave the nation its name), Uri (traditionally Tell's birthplace), and Unterwalden declared themselves independent, forming a defense alliance later joined by Zurich, Lucerne, Berne, and Zug. When Leopold of Austria invaded in 1315 with an army of c.9,000 men, c.1,500 mountaineers ambushed his force in a pass near Morgarten, hurling down rocks and logs, then closing to butcher the disorganized Austrians with crossbow and pike. Further victories over Austrian, Burgundian, and French invaders won Switzerland virtual independence by the end of the 14th century – and established Swiss soldiers as the best in Europe. The Swiss fought on foot in a form of the ancient phalanx, a column some 30 men wide and perhaps 100 deep, armed with 20ft (6m) pikes and halberds (pole axes), with crossbowmen or arquebusiers (hand gunners) in support. By iron discipline and speedy maneuver, they were able to stand against and defeat armored cavalry. Only the development of field artillery at the end of the medieval period broke their domination of European battlefields.

Although Tell may never have existed, a chapel in his honor – site of this modern wall painting showing the hero, with crossbow, escaping Austrian pursuit – at Sisikon, Uri canton, probably dates from the later Middle Ages.

Terrain like this gave the Swiss guerrillas, expert mountaineers, an advantage over conventional troops.

Swiss pikemen hired out all over Europe in the 15th century, when their massed formations dominated many hard fought battles.

❑ The greatest Swiss victory over Austria was in 1386 at Sempach, where c.4,000 Austrians engaged c.1,600 Swiss. Duke Leopold III of Austria ordered his cavalry to fight dismounted and at first drove the Swiss back. But the heavily armored Austrians soon tired and were broken by a fierce counterattack. Leopold and c.2,500 of his men died. One Arnold Winkelried is said to have made the first breach in the Austrian line by charging forward and hurling himself on the enemy's pikeheads.

❑ Most European commanders sought to hire Swiss mercenaries during the 15th century. The price was high, and Swiss soldiers would not fight unless paid in advance. A military proverb warned: 'When the money runs out – so do the Swiss!' Pope Julius II (in office 1503-13) set up the Vatican's famous Swiss Guard (below) – still in existence, and still wearing a colorful ceremonial uniform said to to have been designed by Michelangelo.

Timur: prince of destruction

In the 1370s a descendant of Genghis Khan set out to recover his ancestor's Mongol Empire. In fact, Timur Leng (1336-1405) (Timur 'the Lame;' known in Europe as Tamerlane and in the East as 'Prince of Destruction') was of Turkish-Mongol blood, his kinship with Genghis uncertain. Fighting his way to leadership of the khanates (Mongol states) of central Asia, he made his capital at Samarkand (now in Uzbekistan) after 1361. Timur was a devout Muslim who fought mostly against other Muslims; a savage killer who loved to discuss philosophy and art and made Samarkand an architectural glory. With c.100,000 horsemen (he himself, lame from an early war wound, often traveled in a litter) he swept through Persia (Iran) and Russia, where he defeated the Muslim Golden Horde and thus unwittingly paved the way for a Christian nation. In 1398 he descended on north India, claiming the Muslim Sultan of Delhi was a tool of Hindu infidels, and sacked Delhi so thoroughly (murdering c.100,000 persons) that it did not recover for a century. Taking Indian war elephants (to carry loot; he said that in battle they could be 'driven like cows'), Timur rushed west again, defeating the Mameluke rulers of Egypt in Syria. At Angora (Ankara) in 1402 his horse archers crushed the Ottoman Turkish Sultan Bayezid I's largely dismounted force: Timur's pre-battle capture of the Ottoman water supply persuaded Bayezid's Tatar (Mongol) cavalry to change sides. He might have destroyed the Ottoman Empire, but again he turned restlessly away – to die while marching on China. He only briefly restored Genghis's empire, for he preferred loot and slaughter to statesmanship. Divided among his sons, the huge realm soon fragmented.

The Gur Emir, the magnificent tomb of Timur at Samarkand, was built by his son Shah Rukh, who succeeded to the rule (1405-47) of the central part of his father's empire.

Abstract decoration, in accordance with Muslim law that forbids 'graven images,' covers the tomb.

A Persian miniature of Timur's period shows the hero Bahram Gur. He carries a short, re-curved bow of the type used by Timur's horsemen in the conquest of Persia.

Horse archers in action: a 16th century illustration by an artist of the Mogul (Mughal) regime founded in north India by Timur's descendants.

❑ Timur's path was marked by towers of skulls – the severed heads of his captives. When Isfahan opposed him in 1388 he had c.70,000 citizens beheaded to build his towers; when he besieged Smyrna in 1403 he drove off a Christian fleet by hurling the heads of captives at it from catapults. He sometimes made field fortifications from the living bodies of prisoners, by building them into mud walls.

❑ Timur's hatred of Sultan Bayezid (called *Yilderim*; 'Thunderbolt') was said to stem from Bayezid's claim that Timur had very small sex organs. Captured at Ankara, Bayezid was made to serve as Timur's foot rest at feasts where the Sultan's favorite wives were forced to act as topless waitresses (below). He soon died insane.

❑ Timur's great grandson Babur (1483-1530) conquered Afghanistan and Delhi, and in 1526 founded the Mogul (Mughal) Empire, a Muslim regime that dominated north India until 1857.

The monks of war

The Teutonic Knights' castle at Marienburg, East Prussia (now Malbork, Poland).

The Knights Hospitaller and Knights Templar, founded during the Crusades, were 'fighting monks' who shunned women and wealth, accepted only the Pope as their overlord, and swore always to give battle against Saracens whatever the odds. The Hospitallers were originally civilians who tended sick pilgrims in Jerusalem. In c.1115 nine French knights formed a military monastic order, the Poor Knights of Christ – called Templars from their headquarters in 'Solomon's Temple' (the Dome of the Rock mosque). The Hospitallers followed suit. The two orders were heroic Christian warriors – and deadly rivals. Battles lost and plans frustrated because of quarrels between Templars and Hospitallers contributed to the loss of the Holy Land in 1291. In spite of their monastic vows, both orders amassed treasure, and the Templars acted as bankers and moneylenders. In 1307-12 King Philip IV of France and his puppet Pope Clement V framed the Templars on charges of heresy and vice. The order was suppressed; many knights were tortured and executed; Philip and other rulers grabbed their treasure. Some was given to the Hospitallers, who established an independent state (1310-1522) on the Mediterranean island of Rhodes. A third military order founded in Jerusalem, in 1198, was the Teutonic Knights. All were German noblemen who, after the Crusades, campaigned in the pagan lands northeast of Germany. By c.1400 they ruled an independent state extending from Prussia across Livonia (Estonia, Latvia, Lithuania). They were hated by the Slav peoples, whom they killed or drove out to make way for German settlers. Eastern Europe rejoiced when they were crushingly defeated by King Ladislas of Poland at Tannenberg (Grunwald) in 1410.

Krak de Chevaliers, Syria: the strongest of the Crusader castles in the Holy Land. Completed around 1142, it was garrisoned by Knights Hospitaller, who withstood 12 sieges before the fortress was taken by a ruse in 1271.

From Marienburg, the Knights' Grand Master ruled much of Eastern Europe in the 14th century.

Begun in 1274, the castle declined after the Knights' defeat in 1410. It owes much of its splendor to 19th century restoration.

The castle's store houses and water reservoir could sustain c.2,000 fighting men for long periods.

Soldiers of the First Crusade ride in triumph through Jerusalem: a 12th century wall painting from a chapel built by the Knights Templar.

As seen here, the 'military monks' usually wore light colored mantles over their armor, to deflect the heat of the sun, during their campaigns in the Holy Land.

FACT FILE

❏ Knights Templar claimed they always slept fully armed, and that no knight removed his white mantle with its red cross until it rotted from his back or was slashed away by a Saracen blade. St. Bernard's praise of their unworldiness makes them sound like Hell's Angels: 'You never see them combed; they rarely wash; their beards are bushy, sweaty, and dusty.'

❏ The Templars' seal (below) showed two knights on a horse, one behind the other. They claimed the image stood for brotherhood and poverty; their enemies alleged it was a symbol of homosexual rites that were used in the Order's secret rituals.

❏ Jacques de Molay, last Grand Master of the Templars, was burned to death in Paris in 1314 after long imprisonment and torture. At the stake, he called on Philip IV and Clement V to appear with him before God. Although neither was very old (Philip was 46; Clement about 50) nor ill, both died within a year.

Captains of fortune

The *condottiere* Niccolò Mauruzi da Tolentino, leading Florentine troops against the Sienese at San Romano in 1432, brandishes his commander's baton.

Medieval rulers often hired mercenaries to strengthen their armies, but after 1360 a lull in the Hundred Years War reduced demand for mercenaries' services. Many formed 'free companies:' some simply robber bands; others well-organized private armies. One was the 'White Company' (so named from the cleanliness of its gear, a sign of good discpline) of the Englishman Sir John Hawkwood (c.1320-94). He led his band, about 3,000 strong at peak, into Italy, land of rival city-states, and hired out in turn to Pisa, the Papacy, Milan, and Florence. Hawkwood's huge profits – five cities once paid him 220,000 florins (c.17,200lb/7,800kg of gold) just to leave them alone for five years – inspired Italians to follow suit. The mercenary captains were called *condottieri*, from the *condotta* (contract) drawn up for their employment.

Leonardo da Vinci's design for a flying machine. The 'ornithopter' was intended to have bird-like, flapping wings, driven by a man lying prone along the framework and 'pedaling' with hands and feet.

Among the most successful was Muzio Attendolo (1369-1424), who under his nickname *Sforza* ('Strength') founded one of Italy's most powerful families. His bastard son, the *condottiere* Francesco Sforza, made himself Duke of Milan in 1450. *Condottieri* fought solely for gain, and did not hesitate to break their contracts and change sides for profit. Their battles, unlike their treatment of civilians, were rarely bloody. A *condottiere*'s veteran soldiers were his working capital, and he was reluctant to lose any. Opposing *condottieri* might agree to stage a near bloodless battle to satisfy their employers: the mercenary armies of Milan and Florence fought all day at Molinella in 1427, with only 300 casualties out of 20,000 men engaged. This unreal warfare declined after c.1480, when France and other states began to form 'standing' national armies, full time professional bodies with no place for 'free lances.'

The great Renaissance artist Leonardo da Vinci (1452-1519) won the favor of *condottieri* like Ludovico Sforza of Milan with his designs for weapons and, as seen in this drawing, military fortifications. Among the *condottieri* he served as an engineer and architect was the infamous Cesare Borgia.

The map shows Italy as it was in the mid-15th century: a patchwork of kingdoms, duchies, republics, and city-states. Conflicts between them over territory or trade were frequent – and they often called on the mercenaries led by *condottieri* to fight them. Italy was not united until the 19th century.

Map labels:
DUCHY OF MILAN
DUCHY OF SAVOY
REPUBLIC OF VENICE
Venice
Verona
Padua
Mantua
Milan
Turin
REPUBLIC OF GENOA
Ferrara
Bologna
Rimini
Florence
Urbino
Lucca
REPUBLIC OF FLORENCE
Pisa
Siena
PAPAL STATES
ADRIATIC SEA
CORSICA (GENOA)
Rome
KINGDOM OF NAPLES
Naples
SARDINIA (SPANISH)
TYRRHENIAN SEA
Palermo
SICILY (SPANISH)

The pride and power of a *condottiere* are conveyed in the equestrian bronze by Donatello (1386-1466) of Erasmo da Narni of Padua, who was nicknamed Gattamelata: 'Honey Cat' or 'Leopard.'

Gattamelata got his name from his cunning and ferocity, qualities that were shared by most of his fellow *condottieri*. Yet these ruthless mercenaries and power politicians also encouraged many of the greatest artists of the Renaissance.

FACT FILE

❑ *Condottieri* organized their men in groups of three: a mounted man at arms; his squire; and a spearman or bowman. Each group was called a 'lance.' Thus, a city that hired 300 'lances' got 900 men, at least one-third of them heavy cavalry. Mercenaries who often changed allegiance from one *condottiere* to another were called 'companies of free lances,' from which the modern term 'freelance,' for one who works independently, derives.

❑ Ludovico Sforza (*Il Moro*; 'The Moor') (1452-1508), owed his rule of Milan to his *condottiere* father Francesco. But mercenary soldiers also lost him his dukedom. He hired *condottieri* and Swiss mercenaries to oppose an invasion by King Louis XII of France in 1499. But Louis too had hired Swiss mercenaries – and Ludovico's men refused to fight their fellow professionals. Ludovico was captured and died in prison.

❑ Lucrezia Borgia (1480-1519), daughter of Spanish-born Rodrigo de Borja (1431-1503) and sister of the ruthless *condottiere* Cesare Borgia (1476-1507), was not the poisoner and whore of legend. Her evil reputation came from her use as a political pawn by Rodrigo and Cesare. Rodrigo's cunning won him the papacy, as Alexander VI. His rule ended when he was poisoned, probably by friends of his successor Pope Julius II.

Renaissance: 'rebirth' of learning

The later Middle Ages saw the beginning in Europe of the Renaissance ('Rebirth'), a great upsurge of activity in arts and sciences extending through the late 16th century. The 'rebirth' was that of interest in the classical world of ancient Greece and Rome, inspiring the philosophy of 'humanism.' As its name suggests, humanism saw Man as equally important to God. It was not anti-religious (most learned people relied on the Church as an employer), but tried to reconcile the teachings of pagan philosophers like Plato with those of the Church. The humanist spirit was apparent from the end of the 13th century, notably in the *Divine Comedy* of the poet Dante Alighieri (1265-1321), with its use of everyday language, and in the 'realistic' paintings, approaching three-dimensional perspective, of Giotto di Bondone (1267-1337). The Italian city of Florence, which from the 12th century became Europe's financial center and from c.1430 was ruled by the Medici family of merchant bankers, saw some of the greatest works of the Italian Renaissance. Cosimo de' Medici (1389-1464) encouraged the teachings of classical scholars fleeing the crumbling Byzantine Empire, and the mighty dome of Florence's Cathedral, by Filippo Brunelleschi (1377-1446), was inspired by study of the works of classical architects. Lorenzo de' Medici ('the Magnificent') (1449-92) encouraged, among others, Leonardo da Vinci (1452-1519) and Michelangelo Buonarroti (1465-1564), whose works reflected both classical models and new knowledge of anatomy and optics. The Renaissance gave artists, once near anonymous craftsmen, new status: the best known were idolized like modern football stars – and sometimes got large 'transfer fees' to change patrons.

Florentine 'dictator' Cosimo de' Medici the Elder (1389-1464), seen here on a contemporary medallion, also used his immense wealth to further art and learning.

In spite of war damage and a disastrous flood in 1966, Florence today still preserves much of the beauty it won as the major center of the Italian Renaissance.

The 'realism' of early Renaissance art is apparent in Giotto's painting showing St. Francis preaching to birds.

In the St. Francis Basilica at Assissi, Giotto worked in fresco, an old method of mural art brought to perfection by Renaissance artists.

The Cathedral of Our Lady of the Flower, begun c.1300, got its lovely dome, 138ft (42m) diameter at base, in 1420-36.

Donatello (1386-1466), a pioneer of 'realism' in sculpture, was among the finest Florentine artists.

Because it allowed them to express the triumph of humanity, 'David and Goliath' was a favorite subject for Renaissance artists. Donatello makes David a figure of serenity: even Goliath has a calm beauty.

FACT FILE

❏ The Renaissance was not limited to Italy. One of its major artistic innovations, the development of painting in oils, was the work of Flemish (Belgian) painters such as Jan van Eyck (c.1380-1441). The Dutch humanist Desiderius Erasmus (below) (c.1466-1536) paved the way for the Protestant Reformation (which he himself did not favor) of the early 16th century.

❏ Florence's prosperity was such that its coinage became the standard medium of exchange throughout Western Europe. Its gold florin, first struck in 1252, weighed 0.125oz (3.54g) and remained unchanged in quality until 1533. In 1450 it was valued at nearly £5 ($8) English money – as much as a skilled craftsman might earn in six months.

❏ Among Cosimo de' Medici's bequests to the modern world was one we might have preferred to do without. In 1451 he introduced the *Catastro*, the first effective system of personal income tax.

Printing: the quiet revolution

Legend says the first printed book caused its seller's arrest, when folk accustomed to books hand-copied by scribes denounced multiple identical copies as the Devil's work! The printing press was developed (perhaps invented) in the late 1430s by Johann Gutenberg, a German goldsmith who turned his skills to making printing type. He cast metal punches with the letters of the alphabet, reversed and in relief. This 'movable type' was set up to form text, inked, and mechanically stamped on paper. In 1456 he produced Europe's first complete printed book, a *Bible*, in c.300 copies: the 40 that survive are now among the world's most valuable books. The first English printer was William Caxton (1422-91), a wool merchant who had translated French works into English, perhaps already with an eye on the new printing market. In 1475 he printed his translation of the story of Troy. Based first in Belgium, then in London, he went on to publish 107 titles, some 20 his own translations. Caxton knew his market. He followed fashion, spurning still popular but dated texts like the poem *Piers the Plowman* in favor of equally well-known but more 'modern' works like Chaucer's *Canterbury Tales*. He molded fashion, bringing the literary tastes of the French court to England. His choice of the dialect of London (and the royal court) for his books helped create a 'standard English' language. When Caxton died, his foreman Wynkyn de Worde took over and moved to London's Fleet Street, later famous as the home of English newspapers. Printing had by then become a thriving trade across Europe, producing a 'quiet revolution' by helping to spread the new ideas born in the Renaissance.

Gutenberg's *Bible* was made to look as much as possible like earlier, hand written versions, with Gothic typeface based on the script style of the period and hand-colored decoration.

An apprentice in a 16th century printers' workshop laboriously inks the type.

Caxton's device (printer's mark), based on his initials and the numbers 4 and 7.

❑ Wood block printing (mass production of texts from an inked template) originated in China before the 8th century A.D., from which period date the earliest examples of Chinese, Korean, and Japanese printed religious texts. A recent claim that movable metal type was used in c.1160 at Yonsei University, Korea, to print a 28-page book remains unproven.

Early printing presses were messy machines. The apprentices who collected the printed sheets from the press became so inky that their black faces earned them the name of 'printers' devils.'

❑ Gutenberg developed a special blend of lead, tin, and antimony to cast his type – a mixture easily molded but hardwearing once set. His compound is still used by traditional printers.

❑ Early printers saved a letter by using the symbol 'Y' instead of an older sign (the 'thorn') for the letters 'th.' Thus, the word 'Ye' in mock-antique signs like 'Ye Olde Coffee Shoppe' is not a quaint old usage, but simply a printer's abbreviation of 'the.' The 'long s,' resembling a modern 'f,' remained in use until the 18th century; of course, it was always pronounced as an 's.'

Typesetters had to assemble letters for a few pages at a time, then re-use them – a maddeningly slow process.

❑ Books made in the infancy of printing, before 1500, are called *incunabula* (from Latin *cuna*, 'cradle'). These first printed books imitated hand-copied texts. Typefaces were based on scribes' writing and ornamental capital letters at the beginnings of chapters were colored – first by hand, but from 1457 by the process of three-color printing.

The Duchess Margaret of York, Caxton's patron, accepts a copy of his first book, perhaps from Caxton himself.

Translator Earl Rivers cut this anti-feminist passage from Socrates: publisher Caxton restored it.

Conquerors from Turkey

The peoples of Anatolia (Turkey), unified by Sultan Osman I (ruled 1299-1326), were named 'Osmanli' (Ottomans) in his honor. Osman's *ghazis* (Muslim warriors) swore a *jihad* (holy war) against their Christian neighbors – notably those of the crumbling Byzantine Empire. Ottoman Turkish rule soon expanded into the Balkans and Greece: Sultan Murad I crushed the Serbians at Kosovo in 1389; Bayezid I defeated a 'crusade' led by King Sigismund of Hungary at Nicopolis in 1396. Bayezid's defeat by Timur (*pages 78-79*) temporarily stemmed the Ottoman tide – but it came to flood under Murad II (r.1421-51), creator of the Janissaries (*yeni cheri*: 'new troops'). Every five years the Turks took male children from the conquered Balkans and forcibly converted them to Islam. Nominally slaves, they got privileges in return for absolute obedience. Trained to war from childhood, the Janissaries' iron discipline and weapon skills made them the world's best heavy infantry. Under Muhammad II ('the Conqueror') (r.1451-81) the Ottomans at last took Constantinople, which raised only c.10,000 men against Muhammad's c.70,000 fighters and 70 guns, on May 29, 1453. Eight weeks' bombardment by Turkish guns, some directed by renegade Christians, breached the massive walls; 15,000 Janissaries led the assault; Emperor Constantine XI died heroically in combat. So ended the thousand-year Byzantine Empire; Constantinople, renamed Istanbul, became the Ottoman capital. At the end of the Middle Ages the Turks ruled southeast Europe and much of the Middle East and North Africa. Their onslaught on Europe was checked at Belgrade in 1456 by János Hunyàdi of Hungary and at Vienna in 1529 – but would not end until another defeat at Vienna in 1683.

This magnificently illuminated Ottoman Turkish copy of the *Koran* dates from the 15th-16th centuries. Although an Islamic power, the Ottomans employed non-Muslim mercenaries – notably gunners – in their armies.

A Turkish illustration of the 16th century shows an Ottoman army beginning a march of conquest into Europe. The tall, white headdresses of the bowmen of the commander's bodyguard mark them out as Janissaries.

The map shows the Ottoman Turkish Empire at its greatest extent, following the conquests made by Sultan Suleiman I ('the Magnificent') (1495-1566). Although in decline from the 17th century onward, the Ottoman Empire would remain a significant world power until World War I.

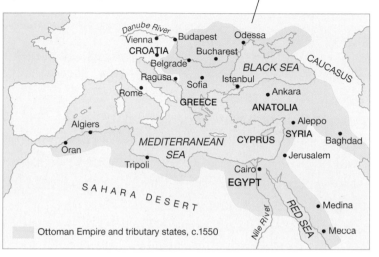

Ottoman Empire and tributary states, c.1550

Like the Janissaries, these horsemen belong to an elite unit, the *Kapikulu*. These *Sipahis* (cavalry; as Spahi the term passed into use with other armies) were a heavily armored strike force in battle.

A Turkish shield from the 16th century: a finely decorated example, probably intended for parade rather than battle.

❑ János Hunyàdi (c.1387-1456), Hungary's national hero, was an early advocate of a paid, professional, 'regular' army on modern lines. But his victory at Belgrade in 1456 was won with the aid of peasant levies led by a Franciscan friar, St. John of Capestrano. In battles against Hunyàdi the Turks learned the effective use of hand gunners and field artillery ('wagon forts'). Hungary finally fell to their onslaught in 1526.

❑ In 1480 Muhammad II laid siege to the island of Rhodes, last Christian stronghold in the east Mediterranean. In its defense by the Hospitallers (Knights of St. John), a weapon based on ancient technology proved superior to Ottoman cannon. The Knights used a trebuchet (above) (a catapult worked by a counter weight) accurately to lob huge stones to a range of 500yd (450m), killing besiegers and collapsing mines dug to undermine the walls. In 1522 another Ottoman siege forced the Knights to abandon the island.

Henry the Navigator, the sailors' prince

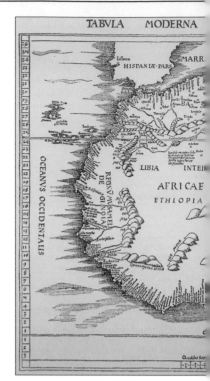

In June 1494 Spain and Portugal signed the Treaty of Tordesillas, dividing between them the 'new lands' of the Americas, Africa, and Asia. Portugal's ability to claim such a huge share of the world owed much to Prince Henry 'the Navigator' (1394-1460), third son of King John I (reigned 1385-1433). Henry himself was a landlubber – a soldier who won territory from the Moors of North Africa – but his patronage laid the foundations of a seaborne empire. After encouraging voyages which opened for settlement the Atlantic islands of Madeira and the Azores, he set up at Sagres a naval academy where the best geographers and mathematicians worked on navigational aids and charts. His shipwrights built caravels, small (c.50 tons), sturdy craft, whose three-masted rig, combining square and lateen (triangular) sails, gave great driving power but could be worked by a small (20-30 man) crew. From c.1430 Portuguese mariners worked their way down the African coast. Trade with Mali (*pages 22-23*) began in the 1440s; by the 1460s caravels were opening up the 'Gold Coast' on the Gulf of Guinea. Gold was not the only lure: in 1444 the first cargo of kidnaped Africans reached Portuguese slave markets. In 1488 Bartholomew Diaz was the first European to round the Cape of Good Hope, proving that a sea lane to the Orient existed around the southern tip of Africa. This 'spice road' was opened by Vasco da Gama, whose caravels reached Calicut (southwest Madras) in India in 1498. Da Gama's later voyages established Portuguese rule at Calicut and in Mozambique, East Africa, where it would last until the 20th century. And in 1500 Portugal gained a massive stake in the 'New World' when Pedro Cabral claimed for her the vast territory of Brazil.

Da Gama died in India, but his body was brought home for burial in Lisbon's Hieronymite Monastery.

A sailing ship is seen on the central panel of the tomb of Vasco da Gama (c.1469-1525), who pioneered the sea way to India round the Cape, opening the way for Portugal to become a great colonial power in Africa and India.

PARAIMOS·NOS·ASSI·DO·SANDIO·AEM

Empty spaces on the map: Europe's picture of sub-Saharan Africa before the voyages of the great Portuguese navigators of the 15th century.

Prince Henry the Navigator: the landsman whose enlightened patronage of his nation's mariners opened up some 1,500mi (2,400km) of Africa's coastline.

❑ Colonization of the Madeira islands (known to the ancients, forgotten, then rediscovered in the 1420s) prospered thanks to an apparent ecological disaster. Attempting to clear the islands' dense vegetation, early settlers started forest fires that raged out of control for seven years. When the fires burned out, the ground was left covered with a layer of potash – which proved an ideal fe rtilizer for vines. Madeira soon became (and still is) famous for fine wines.

❑ Portuguese explorers combed the West African coast for the mouth of the 'Western Nile,' a river leading to the land of 'Prester John.' This mythical monarch (sometimes identified with the king of Ethiopia) was said to be a Christian ruler of immense wealth and power. Many medieval European rulers sent expeditions into Africa to enlist his aid in a crusade against the Muslims – but few of their emissaries to 'John the Priest' were heard of again.

❑ Bartholomew Diaz commemorated the near destruction of his expedition in savage seas by naming Africa's southernmost point *Cabo Tormentoso* (Cape of Storms). King John III, recognizing the commercial possibilities of a sea lane to the Orient and not wishing to discourage other mariners, quickly ordered it renamed *Cabo da Bona Esperanca* (Cape of Good Hope).

Wars of the Roses

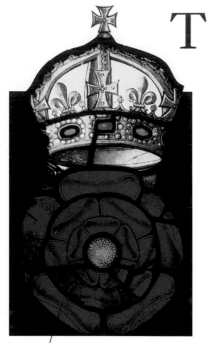

The Wars of the Roses were not truly wars and had little to do with roses. Their name, from the supposed use of red and white rose emblems by the opposing sides, is a 19th century invention. They spanned 30 years, but campaigns occupied only about 3 months of that time. Most battles were fought by small, 'private' armies, and most people were little affected and did not favor either side. Under King Henry VI (1422-71), a weak man dominated by corrupt courtiers and subject to fits of madness, two great families vied for power: Lancaster (red rose) and York (white rose). Henry himself was a Lancastrian, but the real leader of his party was his energetic wife, Margaret of Anjou. The Yorkists were led by Duke Richard of York, who had been recognized as heir to the throne until the birth of Henry's son in 1453. In 1455 Richard rose in arms with the support of Richard Neville, Earl of Warwick, called 'the Kingmaker' from his great power. He defeated and imprisoned Henry and made himself Protector (king in all but name). The Lancastrians struck back in 1460, killing Duke Richard at the battle of Wakefield. But Queen Margaret was a better general than politician: she won battles, but allowed Richard's 19-year-old son to proclaim himself King Edward IV. Edward crushed the Lancastrians at Towton in 1461 and forced Margaret to flee to France. Edward's self-willed behavior angered Warwick, who changed sides. In 1470 Warwick and Margaret invaded from France: Henry VI was restored and it was Edward's turn in exile. Aided by Charles the Bold, Duke of Burgundy, Edward returned in 1471 to smash the Lancastrians at the battles of Barnet (where Warwick was killed) and Tewkesbury. He had apparently established a Yorkist dynasty, but it was short lived.

The red rose, emblem of the House of Lancaster, would become the 'Tudor rose' after the fall of the Yorkist dynasty.

The ill fated Edward, Prince of Wales: his reign as King Edward V would last for only a few weeks.

The crown worn by the monarchs of the short lived Yorkist dynasty.

The white rose, emblem of York, is seen here on a stained glass panel in Gloucester Cathedral.

Yorkist King Edward IV and his family are commemorated in stained glass in England's Canterbury Cathedral.

King Henry VI was ruled by his formidable wife, Margaret of Anjou – seen here receiving a gift from a courtier.

Elizabeth, Edward IV's queen: her eldest daughter's marriage to the future Henry VII would unite York and Lancaster.

FACT FILE

❑ The first rising against Henry VI's misrule was by farmers, tradesmen, and laborers under 'Jack Cade,' who in 1450 led c.40,000 rebels to London. They briefly took control and executed unpopular officials, but dispersed when promised free pardons. Cade (also called 'Jack Amend-All,' from the large promises he made) was killed while resisting arrest. His alias, it is said, came from his invention of a way to preserve pickled herrings in 'cades' (large barrels).

❑ The battle of Towton, March 29, 1461, was perhaps the most savage ever fought in Britain. Yorkists and Lancastrians met in hand-to-hand combat on a Yorkshire hillside in a blinding snowstorm which made neither cannon nor archers of much use. Of c.45,000 men engaged, c.20-25,000 died. The Lancastrians were routed and massacred in 'Bloody Meadow:' a nearby river is said to have run red with blood for 3mi (5km).

❑ Edward IV was a mighty man – at 6ft 4in (1.9m) tall a giant in his time – with a matching appetite for women and liquor. He was also cruel and treacherous: he had his own brother killed; had poor, mad Henry VI and his son put to death after Tewkesbury; and in 1475 took a huge bribe from Louis XI of France (called 'the Spider King' for his vicious intrigues) to desert his former ally, Duke Charles the Bold of Burgundy.

Richard III: monster and murderer?

Drink and women speeded the death at 41 of King Edward IV of England in 1483. His 12-year-old son reigned as Edward V for only a few weeks. Edward IV's younger brother Richard (1452-85), Duke of Gloucester, fearing for England under a boy king dominated by greedy kinfolk, imprisoned Edward V and his younger brother in the Tower of London and took power as King Richard III. Most people accepted him – until rumors spread of the murder of the 'Princes in the Tower.' Many believe that Richard ordered them smothered and buried beneath a staircase – and two skeletons found thus in 1674 (reburied in Westminster Abbey as the princes' remains) are said by modern forensic scientists to be those of boys of the right age. But some say they were killed without Richard's knowledge by the Duke of Buckingham (who hoped to be a new 'Kingmaker'); or by Richard's successor Henry VII. Guilty or not, Richard lost support and his enemies rallied to the exiled Lancastrian Henry Tudor (1457-1509), Earl of Richmond. Henry landed in Wales, and on August 22, 1485, met Richard's army at Bosworth Field. Henry had c.5,000 men; Richard twice as many – but their morale was low. As the battle hung in the balance, Lord Stanley, on whose support Richard relied, changed sides with c.5,000 men. Richard made a desperate cavalry charge and was unseated and cut down. The new King Henry VII united Lancaster and York by marrying Edward IV's eldest daughter. He was a cold, unloved man, but a clever, hardworking administrator, and built a law abiding, prosperous realm. The deaths of so many nobles in the Wars of the Roses enabled him greatly to increase royal authority: his successors in the Tudor dynasty became absolute (all powerful) rulers.

Based on contemporary sources, this portrait of King Richard III shows a calm, thoughtful monarch, with little sign of the supposed deformity that caused his many enemies to nickname him 'Crouchback.'

A 19th century artist shows the 'Princes in the Tower' – King Edward V and his brother Richard, Duke of York – fearfully awaiting their fate. Richard III had them declared illegitimate, but may not have been guilty of their murder.

The first Tudor rulers, Henry VII and (seen here) his son Henry VIII (reigned 1509-47), greatly increased the power of the English monarchy.

After the destructive power struggle between York and Lancaster, most welcomed the stern but comparatively just rule of Henry VII.

FACT FILE

❑ Richard III was not the humpbacked monster portrayed by Shakespeare and other Tudor propagandists. Contemporaries described his 'uneven shoulders,' perhaps because of muscles over developed from daily practice with a heavy, two-handed sword. He was a formidable fighter: one account of his death at Bosworth says that, unhorsed, he fought with '21 tall men,' hacking down many in an attempt to reach the traitor Stanley.

❑ Another crime falsely attributed to Richard III was the murder of his brother George, Duke of Clarence, supposedly drowned in a barrel of Malmsey wine. (It is possible he was drowned in a bath of water, so no marks of violence would show – the Malmsey story was perhaps a cruel joke based on his hard drinking.) In fact, Clarence's killing in 1478 was ordered by his older brother Edward IV, against whom he plotted.

❑ Lambert Simnel (c.1477-1534), a baker's son, was made figurehead of a revolt against Henry VII in 1487. The rebels were defeated and Henry, to show his contempt of Simnel's claim to royal descent (as Clarence's son), made the boy a servant in the royal kitchens. Perkin Warbeck (c.1474-99), who claimed to be Richard of York, younger of the 'princes in the Tower,' was executed after heading revolts in 1495 and 1498.

Spain: kingdom of intolerance

By 1300 Christian reconquest of the Moorish kingdoms of southern Spain reduced the Moors to one realm, Granada. Christian Spain was dominated by two kingdoms, Aragon and Castile. In 1469 the marriage of Prince Ferdinand of Aragon (1452-1516) and Princess Isabella of Castile (1451-1504) signaled the birth of a powerful, united Christian state. Ferdinand II inherited Aragon in 1479, and helped Isabella win a war of succession in Castile. In 1481 the 'Catholic Monarchs' (a title of honor from Pope Alexander VI) agreed to rule both kingdoms jointly. Both were clever statesmen, patrons of the arts, learning, and discovery (Isabella was Columbus's backer) – and religious bigots. In 1478 they persuaded Pope Sixtus IV to authorize the Spanish Inquisition, an 'inquiry' into heresy. Controlled by the crown, not the Church, the 'Holy Office' became a political as well as religious weapon. Its main targets were *Marranos* (Jews who had converted to Christianity; the word means 'swine') and *Moriscos* (converted Muslims), seen as socially undesirable and politically untrustworthy. Those who confessed to heresy, usually under torture, were often burned alive in mass ceremonies called *autos-da-fé* ('acts of faith'); executed or not, their wealth was forfeit to the state. In 1492, when Moorish Granada fell after a 10-year campaign, all Jews were ordered to convert or leave Spain. Some 50,000 converted; c.150,000 fled, including many of the nation's best brains. Ferdinand and Isabella founded Spain's 'Golden Age' as mistress of the New World and leading power in the Old. But they also made it a state where intolerance of religious, ethnic, and cultural differences was seen as a virtue. This inflexibility fatally weakened Spain in the modern age.

The imposing Alcázar (Arabic *al-kasr*; 'the palace') fortress at Segovia, central Spain. Here, in 1474, Isabella was proclaimed queen of Castile, which she would unite with her husband's kingdom of Aragon to form a great Catholic power.

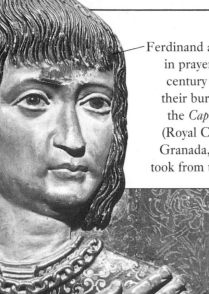

Ferdinand and Isabella in prayer: a 15th century relief at their burial place, the *Capilla Real* (Royal Chapel) at Granada, city they took from the Moors.

❏ The city of Granada, capital of the Moorish state, was defended by massive walls studded with more than 1,000 towers. But it was starved out by the Spaniards in a 10-month siege and surrendered by King Abdallah (Boabdil) (below) in January 1492. The hill from which weeping Boabdil, sent into exile, looked his last on Granada is still called *El ultimo suspiro del Moro* ('last sigh of the Moor').

❏ The Dominican friars of the Inquisition were so zealous in tracking down heretics that they were called, in a Latin pun, *Domini canes* ('God's hounds').

❏ The Spanish Dominican Tomás de Torquemada (1420-98), appointed Grand Inquisitor in 1483, made his name a byword for merciless cruelty: he is said to have ordered 2,000 executions. Estimates of the total number put to death by the Spanish Inquisition range from only 4,000 to more than 30,000. Almost all died in the first century of its activities: its powers were much reduced in the 1600s, although it was not abolished until 1834.

Holiness surrounds the stern judges in this work by Pedro Berruguete, court painter to Ferdinand and Isabella, the Inquisition's great patrons.

The fires are lit beneath stubborn heretics; and at the scaffold's foot other victims (whose garb shows they have 'repented') await their fate.

New age: 'New World'

Caribbean 'Indians' (as Columbus named them) welcome the Europeans – who were to exploit them unmercifully.

The Middle Ages ended with the 'discovery' of the Americas in 1492. Yet Christopher Columbus (Spanish: Cristóbal Colón) (1451-1506) never fully realized what he had found. Born in Genoa, Italy, Columbus was a professional sailor from boyhood. He was inspired by the African voyages of Portuguese navigators, but believed that a better route to the Orient, avoiding hostile Muslim powers, lay west across the Atlantic. For years he sought backing in France, Portugal, Britain, and Spain. He was refused; not because it was thought he would 'sail off the edge' (most educated folk accepted the Earth was a sphere), but because he claimed that Cipanga (Japan) and Cathay (China) lay only c.2,500mi (4,000km), or 30 days' sailing, west of Spain. His opponents rightly said the Orient was much farther off. At last Ferdinand and Isabella of Spain financed an expedition of three ships – the 85ft (26m) long, 100 ton, *Santa Maria*; the smaller *Pinta* and *Santa Clara* (*Niña*) – and 120 men. On October 12, 1492, after a 35 day voyage with crews threatening mutiny, Columbus made the landfall he expected – not off China, but in the Bahamas, on an island he named San Salvador. He sailed on to Hispaniola (Dominican Republic; Haiti) and Cuba before returning to a hero's welcome in Spain. The 'Admiral of the Ocean Sea' made three more voyages. Desperate for wealth, he was accused of cruelty and rapacity in the settlement he founded on Hispaniola, brought back to Spain as a prisoner, and died a bitter, disappointed man. But his obstinacy, greed, and courage had opened the way to a 'New World' and a new age. Publicity given his discoveries through the new printing press would (for good or ill) encourage permanent European settlement in the Americas.

A near contemporary engraving portrays Columbus's landing in December 1492 on the island he named La Española (Hispaniola; now known as Haiti).

One of many portraits said to be of Columbus. Although he changed the face of the world, surprisingly little is known about his personal life.

A modern reconstruction of the little *Santa Maria*, 100 ton flagship of Columbus's first expedition. She was crewed by only about 40 men.

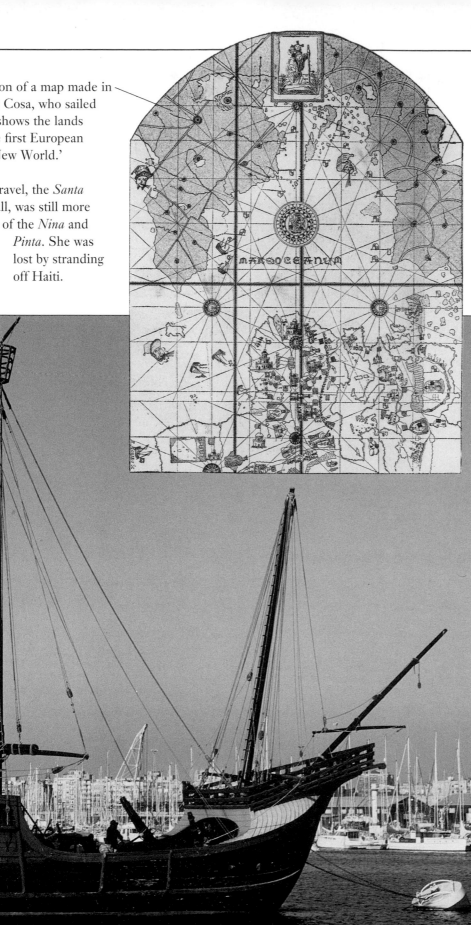

The restored version of a map made in 1500 by Juan de la Cosa, who sailed with Columbus, shows the lands discovered by the first European venturers to the 'New World.'

A three-masted caravel, the *Santa Maria*, though small, was still more than twice the size of the *Nina* and *Pinta*. She was lost by stranding off Haiti.

❑ Until his death, Columbus was certain that the 'Indies' he had found lay off China. The Italian navigator Amerigo Vespucci (1454-1512), who explored the South American coast in 1499-1502, reported that the land was a new continent – and was rewarded by having 'America' named for him. The Genoa-born, British-backed, Giovanni Caboto (John Cabot) (1450-99) had reached Newfoundland and New England in 1497-98.

❑ Celebrations in 1992 of the 500th anniversary of Columbus's voyage were condemned by ethnic and conservationist groups, who denounced him as the forerunner of European colonialism, exploitation, and despoilment of the environment. They had a case. The Indian population of Hispaniola in 1492 is put at up to 3,000,000: some 50 years after Columbus's landfall it was only c.200. Many died of smallpox and other diseases brought by the Spaniards.

❑ Medieval navigation relied on the cross-staff (a simple instrument for taking sun and star sights), astrolabe (a primitive calculator), and, from the 13th century, the compass. Accurate measurement of distance and position at sea depends upon establishing longitude – and this would remain guesswork until reliable lunar tables and marine chronometers (timekeepers) appeared in c.1770-80.

SUPERFACTS

Curse words

A language that has enriched world culture and is still developing dates from around the 10th century, when Jews in the German Rhineland began to develop Yiddish. It probably reflects the tough life of medieval Jews that Hebrew, spoken by all religious Jews for c.4,000 years, has no 'four letter' obscenities: Yiddish has many. Modern Yiddish is c.70 percent German; 20 per cent Hebrew; 10 per cent Polish, Romanian, Russian, Hungarian, and other languages.

Living language

Latin was a universal language for all literate people during the Middle Ages. It remains the official written language of Roman Catholicism, still used conversationally by churchpeople with no common tongue. The Church's most recent Latin dictionary (1992) contains words for such modern objects as U.F.O., dishwasher, and air conditioner. But it does not feature an *exterioris pagine puella* (cover girl) – and its price in *nummus americanus* (U.S. dollars) is extremely high.

Vinland mystery ▼

For years scholars argued whether the Vikings' 'Vinland' was North America. Discovery in 1965 of a medieval map showing North America as '*Vinilanda Insula*' was hailed as clinching evidence – but it proved a forgery. In the late 1950s a Viking settlement of the 11th century was uncovered at L'Anse aux Meadows (below left), Newfoundland. The site does not fit the sagas' description of Vinland ('Wineland,' land of wild grapes), but many now believe Vikings made several expeditions to parts of America.

Miracles: men only ▲

One of medieval England's most popular saints was St. Cuthbert (634-87) (above), whose shrine has been in Durham Cathedral since 995. He was first buried at his abbey at Lindisfarne; then his remains traveled the land with monks fleeing Viking raiders. Opening of his grave in 1827 revealed a carved oak coffin containing his bones and his portable altar, gold and garnet cross, leather-bound Gospels, and woven stole. Like many monks Cuthbert was anti-feminist, and until the 16th century women were barred from his miracle working shrine.

Forkbeard's revenge ▶

Little more than a century after Alfred the Great stemmed Danish invasion, England had a Danish ruler. Sven I 'Forkbeard' of Denmark swore revenge on Ethelred 'the Unready' for ordering the St. Brice's Day Massacre of Danes in England, November 13, 1002, Sven invaded in December 1013. Ethelred fled and Sven proclaimed himself king, but ruled only 40 days before dying of disease. In 1016, after many battles, his son Cnut the Great (c.994-1035) seen here (right) 'ruling the waves,' became undisputed king of England (and later the ruler of Denmark and Norway also).

Alas, al-As!

In 641 Arab general Amr ibn al-As took the Egyptian city of Alexandria from the Byzantines, reporting the capture of '4,000 palaces, 4,000 baths, 400 theaters, 12,000 gardeners, and 40,000 Jews to pay tribute.' No respecter of non-Muslim culture, he fed the 700,000 scrolls of the city's famous library to the furnaces of the baths. The fuel supply lasted six months: the loss of ancient learning was incalculable.

Lost land

The Viking Erik the Red called his new settlement of c.985 Greenland: 'for he said people would be much more tempted to go there if it had an attractive name.' His colony later numbered c.3,000 people. But Greenland's climate worsened and in the 14th century sea ice cut off trade routes. The Western Settlement founded by Erik was wiped out by native Eskimos, whom Norsemen called *skraelings* ('wretches'). In

1406 a Norwegian ship visiting the Eastern Settlement had the last sight of the Greenlanders, who died from starvation and disease later in the 15th century.

Starring role

The law officers of many American communities trace their official title back to Anglo-Saxon England. By the 8th century, an overseer was generally called a 'reeve.' The officers in charge of law enforcement and tax collection in large districts (shires) were 'shire reeves' – a word soon contracted to 'sheriff.'

Crime wave

Medieval Lincoln, England, seems to have been more lawless than a modern inner city. In 1202 (with a population of c.15,000) it saw 114 murders, 164 armed robberies, and 49 rapes. Only two criminals were executed. Some 30 became outlaws after taking sanctuary in churches, but most only had to pay fines.

Fighting mad

Viking warriors called *berserks* (perhaps from *bearsark*, 'bear coat') fought with bestial savagery and might run amok at the slightest provocation. They were generally hated and feared by other Vikings. It has been suggested that their fury was provoked by eating hallucigenic mushrooms; or by 'cabin fever,' a state of irrational violence which affects some people in the northern winters and is still a recognized danger in Alaskan communities.

Counting the hours ▼

Until the 14th century, Western time was generally measured by water clocks or sundials. The first mechanical clocks (i.e., regulated by an escapement mechanism) were built in China, perhaps as early as A.D. 725, and were water powered (below). Europe's first recorded mechanical (weight

driven) clock was built by monks at Dunstable Priory, Bedfordshire, England, in c.1280. At about the same time, the spinning wheel became the first machine to incorporate belt transmitted power in its mechanism.

Blind justice

Byzantine Emperor Basil II *Bulgaroctonus* ('Destroyer of Bulgars') merited his name. In 1014 he defeated Bulgarian attacks on Constantinople, taking c.14,000 prisoners. He ordered them blinded – leaving one man in every hundred with one eye in order to lead the others home. King Samuel of Bulgaria died of shock when he saw his army.

Pulling power ▼

In the 10th century, soon after the appearance of stirrups and nailed, metal horseshoes had revolutionized mounted warfare in the West, another innovation did the same for peaceful use of the horse. The rigid horse collar (below), perhaps developed in central Asia, gave the horse up to five times more pulling power than the earlier chest harness, which had constricted the animal's windpipe.

SUPERFACTS

Seeing things . . . ▲
The English monk Roger Bacon (above) (c.1214-c.1294) was formerly credited with the invention of gunpowder (he appears to have been the first European to record its ingredients), as well as eyeglasses and the telescope. But in Bacon's time the use of magnifying lenses had long been known in China and the West. Spectacles as we know them

probably originated in Italy, where they were first mentioned in writing in c.1290. The first successful telescope did not appear in the West until sometime after 1600.

. . . but not telling
Many medieval legends spoke of Bacon's 'magic arts.' He was said to have constructed a bronze head that would foretell the future. Unfortunately, Bacon was asleep when it came on line. His assistant heard it say 'Time was;' then, 'Time is.' Bacon woke in time to hear it say 'Time's past,' before it shattered into fragments.

Arabian tonic
Ibn Sina (980-1037), also known as Avicenna, was one of the greatest Arab philosophers and scholars; a physician whose *Canon of Medicine* became a standard work throughout medieval Europe. His praise of *bunc*, an infusion of crushed beans, made it a favored tonic in the Arab world. More than 600 years after Ibn Sina's death, *bunc* became popular in Europe – where it is still called coffee.

◄ Dangerous learning
Many medieval men opposed educating women, in case it 'gave them ideas.' Perhaps to support this view, a 13th century Dominican, Steven of Bourbon, invented the story of 'Pope Joan (left).' Joan fell in love with a priest and disguised herself as a man in order to study with him in a religious college. So great was her learning that, as 'Johannes Anglicus,' she became a cardinal and in c.855 was elected Pope John VII – only to be discovered when she gave birth to a child. This ridiculous tale was widely believed and repeated into the 19th century.

Immortal words
A macho slogan of our day was coined by King Richard I of England (below). After a victory in the Third Crusade, he ordered all prisoners killed. His men asked if they should discriminate between Muslims and Christians. 'No,' said Richard, 'Kill 'em all and let God sort 'em out!' He then ordered the bodies cut open, lest some had swallowed jewels or gold for concealment.

Merry monarchs? ▲
Richard I 'Lionheart' fathered only one child (illegitimate) and was rumored gay. Other British rulers were more prolific. Henry I (1068-1135) – called *Beauclerc* ('Good scholar') for his learning – fathered some 20 bastards but left no heir to the throne. Edward I (1239-1307) had most legitimate children of any English king: 19 from two marriages.

Loser in the sex war
Seeking political alliances, Queen Joanna I of Naples (d.1382) married four times. Perhaps disillusioned by her experiences, she once decreed that no man might force his wife to have sex more than six times a day. Men got their revenge: Charles of Durazzo had Joanna killed and took her throne.

Unwelcome invention?
In the late 14th century, a craftsman at Würzburg, Germany, produced the first alarm clock. It was intended for use in monasteries, where monks were obliged to pray at regular hours by both day and night.

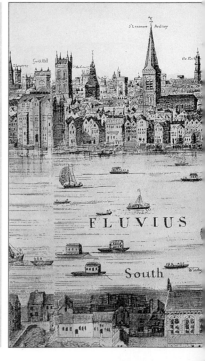

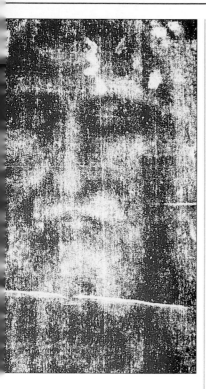

'Holy Shroud' rested in obscurity for many years, to regain fame in modern times as the 'Turin Shroud' (left). Recent carbon dating tests suggest it is a medieval fake – although some say the samples used were too small for accurate testing.

Old London Bridge ▼

The building in stone of London Bridge (below) across the Thames River, replacing a wooden structure of 963-75, was a major feat of civil engineering, which entailed diverting the course of the wide river with coffer dams. Built in 1176-1209, it was London's only Thames bridge – its tolls an important source of revenue – until the 18th century, and was not replaced until the 1820s (by the London Bridge itself replaced in the 1970s and re-erected in Arizona). In 1212, fire among its closely packed shops and dwellings killed c.3,000 people; the city authorities then decreed that London's wooden or thatched roofs must be replaced by tiled ones.

Grave argument ▲

For a sizeable fee, visitors to Lirey, France, in c.1350 were allowed to see a newly found relic: a burial cloth said to have been the winding sheet of Jesus and to bear the imprint of his body. By 1400 Pope Clement VII had condemned it as a fake. The

Millers' tales ▲

The flour mill was a vital resource in medieval communities. Most were water powered, like the one shown (above) in a 13th century manuscript illustration. The windmill, developed in Iran by c.A.D. 650, did not appear in western Europe until c.1180. Millers, comparatively wealthy and powerful men in peasant society, attracted much envy: their alleged lechery and greed is a common theme in medieval literature. A 12th century riddle: Q. 'What is the boldest thing in the world?' A. 'A miller's shirt: every day it takes a thief by the throat!'

Burial – and revival

The great Mongol warlord Genghis Khan died on campaign somewhere in Asia in 1227. He was buried – with many fine horses, 40 beautiful virgins to serve him in the afterlife, and much treasure – on 'God's Mountain,' a site still unidentified. In the 1990s the Genghis Khan Progressive Party got many votes in elections in the Mongolian People's Republic.

Long lasting legislatures

The world's oldest legislative body, or parliament, is said to be the Althing of Iceland, founded c.930. But it was in suspension in 1800-43, so the parliament with the longest uninterrupted existence is the Tynwald of the Isle of Man (in the Irish Sea, and now a semi-independent British possession), founded c.979.

Vital office

A leading official in the British royal household today is the Mistress (or Master) of the Robes. In medieval times the office was termed Groom of the Stole; 'stole' referring not to a robe, but to the monarch's close-stool (portable privy). Where it existed at all, the typical medieval 'john' was a pierced stone slab, perched in an alcove above a castle moat. The close-stool was vital for a traveling monarch's comfort.

Badge of courage

The Knights Hospitaller of the Crusades wore a black mantle with a white, eight-pointed star (said to derive from the flights of four arrows with their points meeting at the center). After 1530 they were called the Knights of Malta, then their headquarters, and their star was known as the 'Maltese Cross.' In tribute to the knights' bravery, it was later adopted as the shape of the German Iron Cross, the British Victoria Cross, and other high awards for gallantry.

SUPERFACTS

Crowned corpse

One of the most hated medieval rulers was King Pedro 'the Cruel' of Castile (1334-69). The murder of his wife, Inez de Castro, on his father's orders, drove him crazy. On becoming king, he had Inez's rotting corpse enthroned at his side and forced his courtiers to kiss its hands. His bloody reign ended when he was defeated and killed in single combat by his brother Henry.

Local hero

England's commonest inn sign is the 'Red Lion.' It has been widespread since the Middle Ages, when it signified the popularity and power of John of Gaunt (1340-99), Duke of Lancaster, fourth son of King Edward III. His heraldic badge was a red lion rampant (rearing up). The world's oldest surviving maker of ale is said to be the Weihenstephan Brewery at Freising, near Munich, Germany, founded in 1040.

Fighting for life

A medieval nobleman accused of a crime might face 'trial by combat,' single combat with his accuser. If victorious, he was judged innocent. In c.1370 a French knight called Macaire was accused of murdering a fellow courtier, Aubry de Montdidier – by Dragon, the dead man's mastiff dog, which persistently attacked him. King Charles V 'the Wise' ordered Macaire to fight the dog. Although armed with a stout staff, Macaire was overpowered. With Dragon's teeth at his throat he confessed the murder and was subsequently hanged.

On the cards ▲

Playing cards, probably originating in China around the 10th century, reached Europe before c.1300. The earliest (Italian) decks were the cards of the Tarot, used for games as well as fortune telling. The modern deck of four suits had evolved by c.1440 – the example (above) is from the 1500s – when the still surviving game of piquet was popular. An English law of 1463 forbade import of 'dyces . . . and cardes for pleiying.'

Accursed name?

England's three kings named Richard all died violent deaths: Richard I of a crossbow wound; Richard II forced to abdicate in 1399 and probably murdered in prison; Richard III killed in battle in 1485. No British monarch has since borne the unlucky name. To luxury loving Richard II we may owe an advance in personal hygiene: he is said to have pioneered the modern use of the handkerchief.

Sporting life

Sports enjoyed by common folk during the Middle Ages included competitive archery, animal fights (particularly cock fighting and bull baiting), various forms of 'club ball' (forerunners of cricket and baseball), and bowling. Falconry and tennis (the kind now called 'real' or 'royal' tennis) were upper class pastimes. Football was banned several times because of hooliganism and damage to property: in 1467 the Scottish parliament banned both 'fute-ball' and 'goff' (golf).

Sea cats

The legend of Dick Whittington, a poor boy who, with the aid of his pet cat, became Lord Mayor of London was immortalized in 19th-20th century pantomimes. The real Whittington was a knight's son who prospered as a merchant, became richer still by marriage, and was Lord Mayor three times between 1397 and 1420. He had several 'cats' – a type of sailing ship in which coal was brought to London; a trade that made Dick rich.

Useful craft

In the 14th century an unknown person – perhaps a woman too poor to buy a weaving loom – invented the craft of knitting, weaving yarn on hand-held, wooden needles. A German altarpiece of the late 1300s shows the Virgin knitting a woolen sweater for baby Jesus, using four needles.

Space suit ▼

The suits of plate armor worn by noblemen in the later Middle Ages were so well articulated (flexibly jointed) that the wearer could run, bend, even do a somersault, with ease. A 15th century French picture (left) shows Joan of Arc in fine plate armor. In the 1960s, U.S. scientists designing a space suit for N.A.S.A. made a special study of medieval armor kept at the Tower of London.

Prophecy fulfilled ▲

Richard II was overthrown by his cousin Henry Bolingbroke, who became King Henry IV (reigned 1399-1413). Henry's reign saw constant rebellion; he quarreled with his son (later King Henry V (above)); and in 1408 contracted a form of leprosy. He hoped to win divine favor by leading a new Crusade, since it was prophesied he would die in Jerusalem. But at the age of 46 he died suddenly of a stroke in Westminster Abbey – while praying in a chapel called the Jerusalem Chamber.

Unlucky lady

In 1396, in a political move for peace in the Hundred Years War, Richard II of England, then 29, married 7-year-old Isabella of Valois, daughter of French King Charles VI. Poor Isabella became a 10-year-old widow when Richard was murdered. Refusing to wed the son of his overthrower Henry IV, she returned to France, married the Duke of Orléans, and died in childbirth aged 19.

End of an ogre?

In 1440 'Bluebeard,' Gilles de Laval, Baron de Rais (Retz), Marshal of France and former comrade in arms of Joan of Arc, was executed by strangling and burning. He admitted the rape and murder of c.150 children. It is possible he was framed by noblemen and clergy who hoped to grab his forfeited wealth, and confessed only because by the law of the time confession and penitence allowed his heirs to keep his estates.

Bloodthirsty prince ▼

Prince Vlad (d.1477), ruler of Walachia (in modern Romania), stoutly defended his land against Turks and Bulgars and became a national hero. But his savage treatment of prisoners and the mode of execution he favored (below) won him the nickname 'Vlad the Impaler.' Because of his bloodthirsty reputation he is sometimes claimed to be the original 'Dracula,' although the vampire legend dates back to the ancient world.

Killer omelet ▲

Some medieval folk pursued the secret of alchemy (above) – the 'magic' art of changing base metals into gold – as stubbornly and expensively as some moderns seek winning systems at casinos. In c.1450, one Bernard of Treviso tried a method that entailed mixing 2,000 egg yolks with olive oil and vitriol (dilute sulfuric acid), cooking the lot over a slow fire for a fortnight, then adding metal to be 'transmuted.' The monster omelet failed to work, so to cut his losses he fed it to his pigs. They all died.

Two-way trade

Columbus's landfall in the Bahamas in 1492 soon led to the near extermination of the native Indians. They had their revenge in one way (possibly two). They introduced Europeans to a 'health giving herb' whose fumes were inhaled through a tube called a *tabaco* – and by the later 16th century the tobacco habit was sweeping Europe. Some scientists believe the Indians infected Columbus's men with the sexually transmitted disease syphilis, a plague in Europe from the 16th century.

The armored knight on his warhorse, the symbol of power and authority in the Middle Ages, is portrayed here on a medieval tapestry.

PICTURE CREDITS

The publishers wish to thank the following agencies who have supplied
photographs for this book. The photographs have been credited by page
number and, where necessary, by position on the page: B(Bottom),
T(Top), L(Left), BR(Bottom Right), etc.

The Ancient Art & Architecture Collection: 5, 8, 11(BL), 20-1, 21(T), 24, 24-5, 25(T), 25(B), 26, 26-7, 29(B), 30, 30-1, 32(T)(B), 32-3(T)(B), 33, 37(R), 40, 41(TL), 43(T), 44-5, 45(T)(B), 47(T)(BR), 48, 48-9, 49(TR), 50-1(T), 51, 52, 52-3, 53(TL), 55(TL)(BL)(R), 56-7, 60, 63(R), 65(BR), 66, 67(R), 68(BR), 72, 73(R), 77(BL)(BR), 78-9, 81(BL)(BR), 84, 87(BL)(TR), 88, 89(L), 90-1(T)(B), 92(TL)(BR), 92-3, 94, 94-5, 95(T)(BR), 97(T), 98-9, 100(R), 101(TL)(BR), 103(TR), 104(TL), 105(TL)(B), 107

Art Resource: 2-3, 10, 11(TR), 12(TL)(BR), 13(R), 14(TR), 15, 16, 17, 19(L)(R), 20, 21(B), 28-9, 29(T), 31(R), 38, 40-1, 42, 46, 50, 50-1(B), 54, 56, 57(BL)(TR), 61(R), 63(L), 64, 65(TL)(R), 67(TL), 68(TL), 69(L)(BR), 70, 71, 73(BL), 74, 74-5, 75(T),

79(BL), 82(TL)(TR)(BL), 82-3, 85 (TL)(R), 88-9, 89(R), 91, 97(B), 98(BL), 102(R), 104(BR), 110-11

The Bettmann Archive: 44, 59(B), 75(B), 79(BR), 98(TR), 99

Envision: 14-15, 23(L), 27(R), 36-7, 96-7

F.P.G. International: 77(T)

The Granger Collection: 6, 11(BR), 13(L), 14(BL), 27(L), 31(L), 49(B), 57(TL), 60-1, 62, 72-3, 85(BR), 86-7, 101(B), 102 (TL)(BL), 102-3, 103(TL), 105(TR)

Harvard University Art Museums: 79(T)

Lee Boltin: 22(R), 23(R)

Nordfoto: 70-1

Nordiske Pressefoto: 41(TR), 59(T)

North Wind Picture Archives: 58-9(T), 61(BL), 86, 87(BR), 93, 97(R)

Novosti/Sovfoto: 64-5

Pap/Eastfoto (Sovfoto): 80-1(T)

Photo Researchers, Inc.: 7, 16-17, 18, 22(L), 34, 35(T)(B), 38-9(T)(B), 41(B), 42-3, 43(B), 47(BL), 53(TR), 54-5, 58-9(B), 80-1(B), 84-5, 100(L)

Shashinka Photo Library: 36, 37(BL)(BR)

Swiss National Tourist Office: 76, 76-7

Map artwork on pages 18, 23, 27, 28, 31, 46, 49, 63, 83, and 89 by Peter Bull